Jigsaw

Insightful Reading to Successful Writing

Robert Hickling
Jun Yashima

NATIONAL
GEOGRAPHIC
LEARNING

Australia · Brazil · Mexico · Singapore · United Kingdom · United States

Jigsaw—Insightful Reading to Successful Writing

Robert Hickling / Jun Yashima

© 2020 Cengage Learning K.K.

Photo Credits:
Cover: © Frans Lanting/National Geographic Creative; 9: © stock.adobe.com; 10: © stock.adobe.com; 15: © stock.adobe.com; 16: © stock.adobe.com; 21: © stock.adobe.com; 27: © AFP/COLLECTION CHRISTOPHEL; 28: © stock.adobe.com; 33: © AFP/PHOTO12; 34: © stock.adobe.com; 39: © AFP/PHOTONONSTOP; 40: © stock.adobe.com; 45: © stock.adobe.com; 46: © stock.adobe.com; 51: © AFP/NURPHOTO; 52: © stock.adobe.com; 57: © stock.adobe.com; 58: © stock.adobe.com, 63: © stock.adobe.com; 64: © stock.adobe.com; 69: © stock.adobe.com; 70: © stock.adobe.com; 75: © AFP/NASA; 76: © NASA Image Library; 81: © AFP/BIOSPHOTO; 82: © stock.adobe.com; 87: © stock.adobe.com; 88: © stock.adobe.com; 93: © AFP/COLIN O'BRADY; 93: © AFP/COLIN O'BRADY

For permission to use material from this textbook or product, e-mail to **eltjapan@cengage.com**

ISBN: 978-4-86312-369-4

National Geographic Learning | Cengage Learning K.K.
No. 2 Funato Building 5th Floor
1-11-11 Kudankita, Chiyoda-ku
Tokyo 102-0073
Japan

Tel: 03-3511-4392
Fax: 03-3511-4391

はしがき

　本書は、大学生が英語で情報や考えなどを的確に理解したり、適切に伝えたりできるようになることを目的に作られた、リーディングとライティングの統合型テキストです。

　グローバル化の進む現代社会では、英語で情報や意見を交換し、コミュニケーションを図ることがますます多くの場面で求められており、そのような状況に鑑みて、英語教育も受容能力だけでなく発信能力やコミュニケーション能力の育成も重視するようになりました。

　「発信能力」や「コミュニケーション能力」というと、英会話を思い浮かべる人も多いと思われますが、実際には私たちが日常で情報を得たり、発信したりする大部分は文字を中心として行われています。SNS やメールでのやりとりなどを思い浮かべてみると、現代社会においてコミュニケーションがいかに読むことと書くことに支えられているかがわかると思います。そして、情報を発信する能力とは、単に自分の考えたことや思ったことを雑然と記述する能力のことを意味するわけではありません。メールにせよ、ブログにせよ、ビジネス文書にせよ、文字を通じて情報を効果的に発信するには、書き手の目的や意図が読み手に正確に伝わるように書く必要があります。

　本書がリーディングとライティングの統合型教材である理由は、手本となるリーディングをもとに文章構成や表現方法を学び、それをライティングによって実践して身につけることこそが、グローバル社会において求められる英語力を育成する最も効果的な方法だと考えているからです。

　英語のライティングには、情報伝達の目的や意図に応じた典型的なパターンがあります。本書は、そのパターンに従ったパッセージを手本として、文章構成や表現方法をリーディングから学び、最終的に学習者自身が情報発信の目的や意図に応じて英語で文章を書けるように、センテンスからパラグラフまで段階的にライティングの練習をする構成になっています。多岐にわたる内容のリーディングを題材に、様々な表現方法やパラグラフ構成を学び、それらをライティングで実践しながら身につけることによって、読解力と表現力を同時に磨くことができるように工夫してあります。

　このテキストを通じて、学習者が自信を持って英語で情報や意見を交換し、積極的にコミュニケーションを図れるようになることを願っております。

著者一同

Unit	Title	Writing Purpose
1	Things Happen for a Reason	Cause & Effect
2	Same or Different?	Compare & Contrast
3	Here's What I Think	Giving an Opinion
4	Sorting Things Out	Classification Writing
5	Step by Step	Describing a Process
6	Feeling Through Your Senses	Descriptive Writing
7	Don't You Agree?	Persuasive Writing
8	You Be the Judge	Writing to Evaluate
9	Two Sides to Every Story	Pros & Cons
10	A Bit of Advice	Writing to Advise
11	Please Don't Misunderstand	Writing to Clarify
12	Revisiting the Past	Reflective Writing
13	Seeking Solutions	Problem Solving
14	Let Me Entertain You	Writing to Entertain
15	Positive Impact	Writing to Inspire

各ユニットは 6 ページ構成です。以下に、それぞれの項目やアクティビティの目的と使い方を説明します。

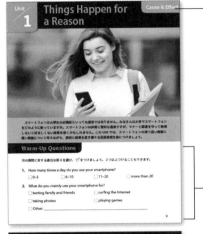

Writing Purpose

各ユニットで学習する文章のパターンが提示されています。
Reading の文章はそのパターンにそって書かれ、最終的にそのパターンのパラグラフが書けることを目標にしています。

Warm-Up Questions

Reading のトピックに関係する質問に答える問題です。英文を読む前に、トピックに対する問題意識を高めます。

Reading

各ユニットの **Writing Purpose** にそって書かれた約 300 語の英文を **Writing Purpose** を意識しながら読みます。様々なトピックについて書かれた英文を読むことで、視野を広げることができます。音声 を聞いて、より深い内容理解をめざします。

Comprehension Questions

本文の内容理解を確認する 3 択問題です。本文の重要ポイントの理解を深めます。

Guided Summary

本文の要約文の空欄補充問題です。本文に出てきた語句を使って、要約文を完成させます。本文の深い理解をめざします。完成したら、要約文を音声 で確認することができます。

Writing Strategy

英語で文章を書く際に、理解して使えるようになってほしい重要項目を、例文をあげて解説しています。そのユニットの **Reading** で、よく使われている項目が取り上げられているので、本文でどのように使われているか、振り返ってみることが大切です。

Check Your Understanding

Writing Strategy で学習した項目に関する選択式問題で、基本的な学習項目の確認をします。

Sentence Writing

A **Writing Strategy** で学習した項目に関する書き換え問題です。学習した項目をマスターするための練習をします。

B **Writing Strategy** で学習した項目を含んだ英文を、自分で内容を考えて完成させる問題です。学習した項目を自分で使えるようになるための練習です。

Paragraph Writing

A 4つの英文を並び替えて、1つのパラグラフを作る問題です。各ユニットの **Writing Purpose** にそって書かれたパラグラフができあがります。**Writing Purpose** の特徴を理解するのに役立ちます。できあがったパラグラフを音声 で確認することができます。

B **Writing Purpose** にそったパラグラフを書くための練習です。条件やヒントが提示してありますので、それに従って書くことにより、**Writing Purpose** にそったパラグラフが書きやすくなっています。パラグラフを書き上げると、各ユニットの目標が達成できます。

音声ファイルの利用方法

 のアイコンがある箇所の音声ファイルにアクセスできます。

https://ngljapan.com/jigsaw-audio

① 上記の URL にアクセス、または QR コードをスマートフォンなどのリーダーでスキャン
② 表示されるファイル名をクリックして音声ファイルをダウンロードまたは再生

Things Happen for a Reason

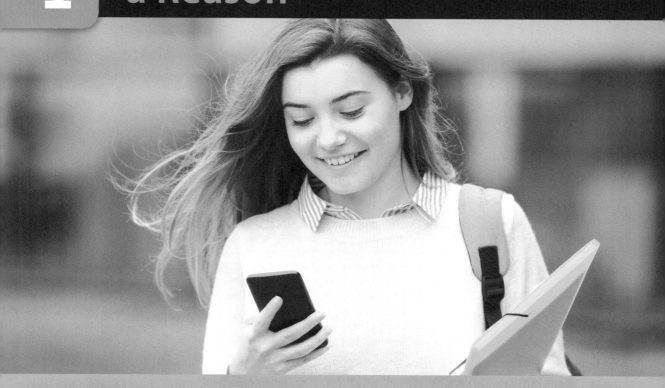

　スマートフォンは大学生の必携品といっても過言ではありません。みなさんは大学でスマートフォンをどのように使っていますか。スマートフォンは非常に便利な道具ですが、マナーと節度を守って使用しないと好ましくない結果を招くかもしれません。この Unit では、スマートフォンの持つ良い側面と悪い側面について考えながら、原因と結果を表す様々な英語表現を身につけましょう。

Warm-Up Questions

次の質問に対する適当な答えを選び、☑をつけましょう。2つ以上つけることもできます。

1. How many times a day do you use your smartphone?

☐ 0–5　　　　　　☐ 6–10　　　　　　☐ 11–20　　　　　　☐ more than 20

2. What do you mainly use your smartphone for?

☐ texting family and friends　　　　☐ surfing the Internet

☐ taking photos　　　　　　　　　　☐ playing games

☐ Other: _____

The Effects of Smartphone Use on University Students

1   One of the most important possessions of a university student, if not *the* most important possession, is their smartphone. Along with textbooks, notebooks and other school supplies, almost every student brings their trusty phone with them when they make the daily trip to campus. It's the one thing they never
5▶ want to leave home without. But what are the effects of smartphone use on university students?

2   First of all, smartphones are, of course, very convenient. Because of smartphones, students can find information quickly, and they never have to look for a pay phone or wonder where their friends are. They can take high-quality pictures easily and share
10▶ them with family and friends. Smartphones also provide Internet access, so students can register for classes online, access their university website and gather information for academic papers—anywhere and anytime.

3   On the other hand, smartphones can be a serious distraction in the university classroom. It is becoming increasingly common for students to text friends or surf
15▶ the Net instead of listening to lectures, taking part in group activities, or completing in-class assignments. As a result, this type of behavior often negatively affects students' academic performance and prevents them from learning. Smartphone addiction may also have destructive consequences. A recent study found that four out of five university students experienced panic, isolation and stress when they didn't have
20▶ access to their smartphones even for one day.

4   In conclusion, smartphones can be great information and learning tools for students, but they may also distract them from learning and cause destructive results. Therefore, it is important for students to take advantage of the opportunities that smartphones offer, while using them in a mature and responsible way.

Notes   trusty 頼りになる   pay phone 公衆電話   distraction 気を散らすもの、注意散漫   addiction 依存、中毒

Comprehension Questions

本文の内容に関して、次の質問の答えとして適当なものを選びましょう。

1. What is one stated advantage of smartphones?

   a. easy access to information   b. low cost   c. compact size

2. What is one result of smartphone use in the classroom that is described?

   a. sleepiness   b. increased academic performance   c. reduced learning

3. What destructive consequence of smartphone addiction is mentioned?

   a. violence   b. mental pressure   c. eye damage

Guided Summary 03 Audio

本文の語句を使って、次の要約文を完成させましょう。完成したら、音声を聞いて確認しましょう。

The one thing that university students never want to leave behind is their

1 _____ . Smartphones are very 2 _____.

They allow students to find 3 _____ quickly, take excellent

pictures, 4 _____ for classes online, and so on. However, smartphones

can be a major 5 _____ in the classroom, where many

students text friends or 6 _____ the Internet. This often affects their academic

performance or 7 _____ them from learning. Smartphone

8 _____ may also result in panic, isolation and 9 _____.

Because smartphones can have both positive and negative effects, it's important to

use them in a mature and 10 _____ manner.

11

Writing Strategy

原因・理由を表す表現

(1) 前置詞として働くもの（due to, because of, owing to など）

後ろに名詞を伴い、原因・理由を表す句を作ります。

- Our flight was delayed **due to** technical difficulties.

  結果　　　　　　　原因・理由

(2) 接続詞として働くもの（because, since, as など）

原因・理由を表す節を作り、主節の内容の原因・理由を示します。

- We had to make a detour **because** the street was closed for repairs.

  結果　　　　　　　原因・理由

結果を表す表現

(1)（等位）接続詞として働くもの（so）

接続詞の後に続く文が前文の内容の結果を表します。文と文を直接結びつけることができます。

- I didn't have an umbrella with me, **so** I got wet.

  原因・理由　　　　　　　結果

(2) 副詞（句）として働くもの（therefore, consequently, as a result など）

副詞（句）を含む文が前文の内容の結果を表します。それ自体では文と文を直接結びつける働きはしません。

- The plan failed. **As a result**, the company's debt has ballooned.

  原因・理由　　　　　　　結果

Check Your Understanding

下の囲みの中の語句から適当なものを選んで、次の英文を完成させましょう。

> because of　　　since　　　consequently

1. (   ) I had a headache, I left the office early.

2. Mary wasn't able to attend the seminar (   ) her late arrival.

3. Bob failed to submit the document. (   ), his application was rejected.

Sentence Writing

A （　　）内の語句を使って、次の英文を１つにつなげてみましょう。

1. Joe forgot to set his alarm last night. Joe was late for work this morning.（**because**）

   Because _____ , _____

   _____ .

2. I couldn't buy the jacket. I didn't have enough money. (**so**)

   _____ , so _____

   _____ .

3. The weather was bad. The game was canceled. (**due to**)

   Due to _____ , _____ .

4. Kate received her driver's license. Kate passed her driving test. (**; therefore,**)

   _____ ; therefore, _____

   _____ .

B 原因と結果の関係がわかるように、自分で自由に考えて次の英文を完成させましょう。

1. Bruce never eats breakfast, so _____

   _____ .

2. Due to the typhoon, _____

   _____ .

3. _____

   _____ . As a result, I was late for class.

4. _____

   _____ . Consequently, the teacher became angry.

Paragraph Writing

A 次の英文を並べ替えて、1つのパラグラフができるように、適切な番号を下の欄に書いてみましょう。書いたら、音声を聞いて確認しましょう。

1. This is mainly due to the invention of the television and other modern technologies such as video games and smartphones.

2. Therefore, parents need to monitor their children's access to technology and pay attention to how it's affecting their lives.

3. As a result of these inventions, children aren't exercising as much as they used to, and they're communicating less with their parents.

4. More than ever before, people have been staying indoors, especially children.

B スマートフォンのマナー違反が原因で起こりうる良くない結果について自分で自由に考え、以下のパラグラフを完成させましょう。

Most people carry their smartphones with them wherever they go. Unfortunately, however, they do not always exercise good smartphone manners. Let's look at two examples of poor smartphone etiquette and the possible consequences. First, _____

_____

_____

_____

_____

In conclusion, _____

_____

Same or Different?

　健康を保つ上で、栄養バランスのとれた食事を取ることは非常に重要です。鶏肉と魚はいずれも栄養価の高い食材ですが、具体的にどのような点で健康食として優れているのでしょうか。この Unit では、鶏肉と魚が他の食材に比べて優れている点やそれぞれに含まれる栄養素ついて述べた文章を読み、比較・対照を表す様々な英語表現を身につけましょう。

Warm-Up Questions

次の質問に対して **1.** では英語で答え、**2.** では適当な答えを選び、☑ をつけましょう。

1. What did you eat yesterday …

… for breakfast? _____

… for lunch? _____

… for dinner? _____

… between meals? _____

2. Do you eat healthy food?　　☐ usually　☐ often　☐ sometimes　☐ seldom

Chicken or Fish?

1 When it comes to eating healthy food, most people know the basic rules—don't eat too many sweets, avoid unnecessary fat, and stay away from junk food. How about chicken and fish? Which one is better for you?

5▶ **2** Most health books and Internet sites will tell you that both chicken and fish are healthy choices in a balanced diet. According to the American Heart Association, chicken and fish are healthy alternatives to red meat as far as heart health is concerned. Compared to beef and pork, they contain less cholesterol and saturated fat, which, if eaten in excess, can increase your blood pressure and cause 10▶ heart problems. Of course, a plate of baked fish or skinless chicken with steamed vegetables is always preferable to a basket of fried chicken or fish and chips.

3 Chicken has long been the white meat of choice for healthy eaters because it's high in protein and low in fat. A 120-gram serving contains about 27 grams of protein, more than almost every kind of fish. Chicken is also one of the most 15▶ affordable kinds of meat in the supermarket. People who hope to stay healthy, slim down, build muscle, or avoid a family history of heart problems will likely have lots of chicken in their diet.

4 The biggest advantage of fish over other protein sources is its high level of omega-3 fatty acids, which the body needs but doesn't produce naturally. Omega-3s 20▶ are believed to improve memory and overall brain function. That's why fish is often called "brain food." Fish also helps prevent heart disease. And although the protein content of fish isn't as high as chicken, many popular kinds will easily help you reach your protein intake for the day.

5 So the next time you're deciding between chicken and fish, take your pick—both 25▶ are smart and healthy choices.

Notes cholesterol コレステロール saturated fat 飽和脂肪 affordable 手頃な価格の
omega-3 fatty acids オメガ3脂肪酸 take your pick 好きなものを選ぶ

Comprehension Questions

本文の内容に関して、次の質問の答えとして適当なものを選びましょう。

1. What is an advantage of chicken and fish over red meat?

   a. higher cholesterol content   **b.** more protein   **c.** fewer heart risks

2. In what way is chicken better than fish?

   a. It's higher in protein.   **b.** It prevents heart disease.
   c. It's easier to prepare.

3. Why is fish often called "brain food"?

   a. It helps make brain cells.   **b.** It improves memory and brain function.
   c. It increases the body's production of omega-3 fatty acids.

Guided Summary

本文の語句を使って、次の要約文を完成させましょう。完成したら、音声を聞いて確認しましょう。

Chicken and fish are both healthy choices in a balanced ⒈_____. Compared to red meat such as beef or pork, they contain less ⒉_____ and saturated fat, both of which can lead to high blood ⒊_____ and heart problems. Chicken is high in ⒋_____ and low in ⒌_____, and it's one of the most ⒍_____ kinds of meat that you can buy. Fish contains less protein than chicken, but its high concentration of omega-3 fatty ⒎_____ is likely responsible for improving ⒏_____ and ⒐_____ function. For this reason, fish is often called "brain food." Fish also helps prevent ⒑_____ disease.

Writing Strategy

比較級を用いて比較を表す

比較級を用いる場合、比較の対象は than ～で表します。

- Your room is **larger than** mine.

比較級を用いないで比較を表す

(1) 動詞自体に比較の意味が含まれるもの

prefer ... to ～（～よりも…を好む）

survive ～（～よりも長生きする）

outweigh ～（～よりも重い、～よりも重要である）

surpass ～（～よりも勝る）、exceed ～（～よりも上回る）など

- The advantages **outweigh** the disadvantages.

(2) 形容詞自体に比較の意味が含まれるもの

(be) preferable to ～（～よりも望ましい）　(be) superior to ～（～よりも優れている）

(be) inferior to ～（～よりも劣っている）など

これらの形容詞を用いる場合、比較の対象は to ～で表します。

- This machine **is superior to** its predecessors.

(3) 原級比較の否定

as ... as ～「～と同じくらい…」を否定すると、「～ほど…ではない」という比較の意味が出ます。

- In Japan, basketball is **not as** popular **as** baseball.
  = In Japan, baseball is more popular than basketball.

Check Your Understanding

下の囲みの中の語句から適切なものを選んで、次の英文を完成させましょう。

better	superior	prefer

1. I much (　　　　　　) Mozart to Bach.

2. This product is (　　　　　　) in quality to all others.

3. He is (　　　　　　) at speaking Spanish than I am.

Sentence Writing

A （　）内の指示に従って、次の英文を書き換えてみましょう。

1. I like playing sports better than watching them. (**I prefer** で始めて)

   _____

   _____

2. Silver is not as heavy as gold. (**Gold is** で始めて)

   _____

3. There is nothing as important as friendship. (**Friendship is more** で始めて)

   _____

   _____

4. She survived her husband. (比較級を用いて)

   _____

B 自分で自由に考えて次の英文を完成させましょう。

1. When it comes to _____,

   I prefer _____ to _____.

2. I think _____

   is more valuable than _____.

3. _____ are much healthier than

   _____.

4. _____ isn't as important as

   _____ in life.

Paragraph Writing

A 次の英文を並べ替えて、1つのパラグラフができるように、適切な番号を下の欄に書いてみましょう。書いたら、音声を聞いて確認しましょう。

1. In contrast, green tea leaves are steamed or pan-fried to prevent fermentation and are much lighter in color than black tea leaves.

2. To make black tea, the leaves are first rolled and then exposed to air, allowing the fermentation process to take place and causing the leaves to turn dark brown.

3. It surprises some people new to tea that green tea and black tea come from the same plant.

4. The difference between the two is that black tea is fermented and green tea is not.
   Note: fermented 発酵した

B ペットとして飼う場合の猫と犬を比較し、以下のパラグラフを完成させましょう。ただし、自身の意見や好みではなく、客観的な記述をしましょう。

Cats and dogs are the most popular pets in the world, and Japan is no exception. I would

like to discuss some similarities and differences between them. First, _____

_____

_____

_____

On the other hand, _____

_____

_____

_____

Here's What I Think

　旅行には、旅行業者が予め旅程を組んだガイド付きのツアーと自分で旅行の目的地や日程を決める個人手配の旅行がありますが、みなさんはどちらが好きですか。どちらにも長所と短所があり、人によって好みも分かれます。この Unit では、旅行のしかたの好みについて述べた文章を読み、英語で自分の意見を提示するのに役立つ表現を身につけましょう。

Warm-Up Questions

次の質問に対して英語で答えましょう。

1. Where in Japan would you like to go? _____

   Why do you want to go there? _____

2. What country would you like to visit? _____

   Why do you want to go there? _____

What's Your Travel Preference?

1   When traveling, some people prefer taking guided tours, while others would rather travel independently and arrange everything themselves. There are, of course, advantages and disadvantages to each type of
5► travel, but in my opinion, independent travel is the way to go for two main reasons described below.

2   First, independent travel gives you the freedom to make your own itinerary—to choose exactly where you want to go and what to do. It also allows flexibility to change the plan at any time, according to the weather, your health
10► condition, your mood and so on. From my experience, these kinds of unplanned adventures often turn out to be the best ones.

3   The second reason why I prefer independent travel to guided tours is because it gives you complete control over how you spend your time. Guided tours are generally very rigid. A fixed amount of time is allotted for each place visited, and
15► everyone is expected to return to a predetermined location by a certain time. It's true that this may work for some people, but it seems to me that a two-hour visit to a museum would be too short for some people and too long for others. Moreover, guided tours are generally organized to show you as many places as possible in a relatively short period of time. While this may appeal to people with limited vacation
20► time, I don't think you can really soak up a city that way. It's hard to imagine traveling all the way to Paris on a guided tour, only to visit the Eiffel Tower and the Louvre Museum.

4   I admit that guided tours are a safe, easy and hassle-free way of traveling. However, independent travel lets you control your itinerary and time and, personally,
25► I wouldn't want to travel any other way.

Notes ▶ the way to go 最良の選択肢   itinerary 旅程   predetermined 予め決められた   soak up 吸収する、浸る
hassle-free 手間のかからない

Comprehension Questions

本文の内容に関して、次の質問の答えとして適当なものを選びましょう。

1. What does the author like about independent travel?

   a. It's flexible.   b. It has a fixed itinerary.   c. It's hassle-free.

2. What does independent travel often lead to?

   a. difficulty in finding hotel rooms   b. unplanned adventures
   c. long waiting times

3. What does the author think about most guided tours?

   a. They're poorly organized.   b. They're not safe.   c. The schedules are tight.

Guided Summary

本文の語句を使って、次の要約文を完成させましょう。完成したら、音声を聞いて確認しましょう。

Some people like to take ___¹___ tours; others prefer to travel ___²___. With independent travel, you have the freedom to decide your own ___³___ and the ___⁴___ to change your plans according to the weather, your health ___⁵___ and your ___⁶___. The author thinks that the resulting ___⁷___ adventures end up being the best ones. Independent travel also lets you decide how to use your ___⁸___. Guided tours, on the other hand, are very ___⁹___. The author believes it's difficult to ___¹⁰___ up a place when your time is limited and the locations you visit are all decided in advance.

23

to 不定詞の用法

（1）名詞的用法

「〜すること」という意味の句を作り、主語、目的語、補語になります。

- I forgot **to bring** my health insurance card. — to bring は forget の目的語

（2）形容詞的用法

「〜するべき」「〜するための」という意味の句を作り、前の名詞を修飾します。

- What's the best way **to learn** a language?

（3）副詞的用法

動詞や形容詞を修飾し、目的、結果、感情の原因、判断の根拠などを表します。

- She went to the library **to return** the book. — 目的

- James did his best, only **to fail**. — 結果

疑問詞＋不定詞

< what/which/where/when/how ＋ to 不定詞＞で、「（何を / どちらを / どこで / いつ / どのように）〜すべきか」という意味の名詞句を作ります。

- I don't know **what to say.**

Check Your Understanding

（　）の中から適切な語句を選び、○で囲みましょう。

1. We discussed ways to (improve / improving) work efficiency.

2. I'm used to (speak / speaking) in public.

3. They launched a new campaign to (attract / attraction) more tourists.

4. I look forward to (see / seeing) you soon.

Sentence Writing

A (　　) 内の指示に従って、次の英文を書き換えてみましょう。

1. This question is so difficult that I cannot answer it. (**too difficult** を用いて)

_____.

2. It doesn't seem that the professor understands what I want to say.

(**The professor** で始めて)

_____

_____.

3. He asked his mother what he should do first. (**to** 不定詞を用いて)

_____.

4. Thanks to this app, you can edit videos on your smartphone. (**allow** を用いて)

_____

_____.

B 自分で自由に考えて次の英文を完成させましょう。

1. Before you leave for the airport, don't forget to _____

_____.

2. The reason I want to travel to _____ is to _____

_____.

3. When I was a child, I used to _____ and

_____.

4. I think the best way to learn English is to _____

_____.

Paragraph Writing

A 次の英文を並べ替えて、1つのパラグラフができるように、適切な番号を下の欄に書いてみましょう。書いたら、音声を聞いて確認しましょう。

10
Audio

1. It's true that big cities have good public transportation networks, a wide selection of shops and restaurants and more career opportunities than small towns and villages.

2. Most of my classmates want to live in a big city after they graduate, but in my opinion, living in the country is much more desirable.

3. For these reasons, I think that the quality of life afforded by country living outweighs the conveniences and other benefits that city living has to offer.

4. However, country life provides plenty of open space, greenery and clean air, not to mention a quiet, relaxing and peaceful environment.

B あなたの一番好きな季節はいつですか。なぜその季節が一番だと思うかについて、自分の意見を付け加えて以下のパラグラフを完成させましょう。

Japan is a country with four distinct seasons, each with its own unique features. In my

opinion, _____ is the best season for several reasons. One reason is _____

_____

Another reason is _____

In addition, _____

But the main reason why _____ is my favorite season is _____

_____

_____

_____

Sorting Things Out

　みなさんはどのような映画が好きですか。映画には様々なジャンルがありますが、どのような映画作品であれ、見た人を満足させられるかどうかがその映画の良し悪しを決める一番の要素だと言えます。その点において映画の結末は作品の最も重要な部分です。この Unit では、映画の結末を 3 種類に分類して説明した文章を読み、分類を表す英語表現を身につけましょう。

Warm-Up Questions

次の質問に対して、**1.** では適当な答えを選び、☑ をつけましょう。2 つ以上つけることもできます。また、**2.** では英語で答えましょう。

1. What kind of movies do you like?

☐ Action ☐ Comedy ☐ Mystery ☐ Science fiction

☐ Romance ☐ Adventure ☐ Horror ☐ Animation

2. Who's your favorite actor, actress, or movie character?

_____

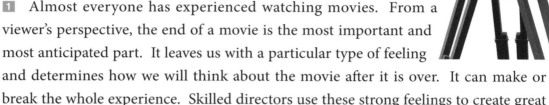

Great Movies Need Great Endings

1   Almost everyone has experienced watching movies. From a viewer's perspective, the end of a movie is the most important and most anticipated part. It leaves us with a particular type of feeling and determines how we will think about the movie after it is over. It can make or break the whole experience. Skilled directors use these strong feelings to create great movies. There are many different types of movie endings, but a great number of them fall into one of three main categories: a happy ending, an unresolved ending and a surprise ending.

2   A happy ending is also called an expected ending. It gives viewers exactly what they want and what they were expecting. Movies about the princess who marries the prince and lives happily ever after, the superhero who defeats the villain and makes the world safe once again, and the protagonist who solves the murder and brings the criminal to justice all fall into this category. By the end of the story, everything is wrapped up, with no unanswered questions. Viewers are left feeling satisfied because the characters end up exactly where they knew they would.

3   An unresolved ending is more commonly referred to as a cliff-hanger. Nothing is resolved and the story's conflicts remain unanswered. The ending forces viewers to rely on their imagination to determine what they think will happen next. It tweaks their curiosity, leaving them wanting more.

4   A surprise ending is also known as a twist ending. As the name suggests, this type of ending comes as a complete surprise to the viewer. A good surprise ending adds a final jolt of unexpected excitement to the movie. Like all other kinds of movie endings, however, if done poorly, it can be a great letdown to an otherwise entertaining story.

Notes   make or break ～の成否を握る   villain 悪者   protagonist 主人公   bring ～ to justice ～を逮捕して裁判にかける
cliff-hanger クリフハンガー（続きを気にさせるような作品）   tweak（刺激して）高める   twist ending どんでん返し

Comprehension Questions

本文の内容に関して、次の質問の答えとして適当なものを選びましょう。

1. What kind of movie ending forces viewers to imagine what will happen next?

   a. a happy ending　　　　**b.** an unresolved ending　　　**c.** a surprise ending

2. What kind of movie ending has no surprises and delivers what viewers expected?

   a. a happy ending　　　　**b.** an unresolved ending　　　**c.** a surprise ending

3. What is another name for a surprise ending?

   a. a twist ending　　　　**b.** a cliff-hanger　　　　**c.** a jolt

Guided Summary

本文の語句を使って、次の要約文を完成させましょう。完成したら、音声を聞いて確認しましょう。

For a movie viewer, the ending is the most important and most ¹_____

part. It leaves us with a strong ²_____ and impression. The three

main types of movie endings are happy endings, ³_____

endings and surprise endings. In a happy ending, everything turns out as

expected. There are no ⁴_____ questions, and viewers

feel ⁵_____. An unresolved ending doesn't answer the story's

⁶_____, forcing viewers to use their ⁷_____

to determine how the story will finally end. An unresolved ending tweaks viewers'

⁸_____ and leaves them wanting more. A surprise ending adds

extra ⁹_____ to a movie, but if done poorly, it can be a real

¹⁰_____.

29

Writing Strategy

受動態

　「（〜は）…される」のように、動作・作用を受ける対象を主語にした形式を受動態といい、＜ be ＋過去分詞 ＞を用いて表します。受動態は常に被害の意味合いを持つわけではなく、客観性の高い事柄を記述する場合にもよく用いられます。受動態では行為の主体は通常＜ by 〜＞で表しますが、受動態の過去分詞が状態を表す場合は by 以外の前置詞も使われることがあります。

- He **was arrested by** the police.
- The story **is known to** everyone.

　行為者が一般的な人を指す場合、また行為者が文脈上明らかな場合や不明な場合などには、受動態が好まれます。その際、＜ by 〜＞はしばしば省略されます。

- Aristotle **is considered** the father of biology.

知覚動詞・使役動詞の受動態

知覚動詞・使役動詞を受動態に書き換える場合、目的格補語の原形不定詞が to 不定詞になることに注意しましょう。

- They made me work until midnight. 能動態
  - ➡ I **was made to work** until midnight (by them). 受動態

Check Your Understanding

（　）の中から適切な語句を選び、○で囲みましょう。

1. The door was (leaving / left) open.

2. He is (thought / thought of) as a great scientist.

3. Titanic was (known / called) the ship of dreams.

Sentence Writing

A (　　) 内の指示に従って、次の英文を書き換えてみましょう。

1. They are investigating the case. (**The case** で始めて)

   _____

2. No one has ever spoken to me like that. (**I have never** で始めて)

   _____

3. We should take care of the issue immediately. (**The issue** で始めて)

   _____

4. They made me wait in the cold for three hours. (**I was** で始めて)

   _____

B (　　) 内の動詞を受動態に変え、質問に答えましょう。

1. Where is your university? (**locate**)

   My university _____

   _____.

2. How old is your university? (**build**)

   It _____

   _____.

3. What is the name of the nearest train or subway station to your university? (**call**)

   The nearest _____

   _____.

Paragraph Writing

A 次の英文を並べ替えて、１つのパラグラフができるように、適切な番号を下の欄に書いてみましょう。書いたら、音声を聞いて確認しましょう。

1. The 20% of the population who are B types are creative and passionate, selfish and uncooperative, while the remaining 10% whose blood type is AB are talented and composed, but are also known to be eccentric and two-faced.

2. First, blood type A people, who represent 40% of the Japanese population, are earnest and neat, but also stubborn and anxious.

3. In Japan, blood types are considered an important indicator of a person's personality, and they may help people make friends and build healthy relationships.

4. Type O people, the second most common group, making up 30% of the population, are easygoing and good leaders, but they can also be insensitive and unpunctual.

B 世界中の人たちが日本に観光に来るのはなぜでしょう。日本に旅行に来る人を４つのグループに分類し、以下のパラグラフを完成させましょう。

I think there are four main types of people who visit Japan. The first group is those who are interested in _____

The second group _____

_____

_____

_____

_____

_____

_____

Step by Step

　日本は言わずと知れたアニメ大国です。世界的にも評価の高い日本のアニメは、脚本から完成にいたるまでに、非常に複雑に細分化された工程を経て制作されています。この Unit では、日本のアニメの制作工程について述べた文章を読み、ものごとの過程や手順を説明するのに役立つ様々な英語表現を学びましょう。

Warm-Up Questions

次の質問に対して、**1.** では Yes または No に☑をつけ、Yes の場合はその後の質問に英語で答えましょう。また、**2.** にも英語で答えましょう。

1. Do you like watching animation?　　　　☐ Yes　　　　☐ No

　　If yes, what's your favorite animation? _____

2. What are the names of some famous animation characters?

　　_____ / _____ / _____ / _____

How Anime Is Made

1　Have you ever wondered how Japanese animation is made? As you can well imagine, it's a complex and painstaking process. It all starts with the script. The script is produced by the artist who develops the original
5▶ animation itself. After being reviewed by the director, it goes into production. Production starts with storyboards. The storyboards include drawings, movements, panning of the camera and the length of each shot.

2　After the storyboards are finalized, layouts for the actual scenery and landscape are drawn on paper and then reviewed. Once the layouts are decided, they go to the
10▶ landscape department, where images are digitally produced.

3　The next step is key animation. Key animators draw the first frame, the middle frame and the last frame of a cut. For example, if character A is going to fall off a cliff, he would be standing in the first frame, falling in the second frame, and then hitting the ground in the final frame. After the key animation is done for every
15▶ frame, in-between animators are responsible for animating the movements between cuts, making the overall animation look smoother and more fluid.

4　After the animators complete their work, the animation goes over to compositing, where all of the coloring and shading is done. A lot of animation companies have entire departments just for the coloring because it's so time-consuming.

20▶ **5**　The final stage of production is effects. The effects department adds the finishing touches which make the animation look truly amazing, by adding everything from shading to smoke to lightning bolts. This is followed by post-production, where voice-overs, sound effects and music are added. Editing is also done so that the anime does not exceed the broadcast time. Some pieces may have to be cut out and
25▶ voice-overs may have to be redone.

Notes　painstaking 骨の折れる　storyboard 絵コンテ　pan パン（パンニングとも呼ばれる映像の撮影技法）
compositing 合成　voice-over ボイスオーバー（アフレコの声）

Comprehension Questions

本文の内容に関して、次の質問の答えとして適当なものを選びましょう。

1. What is NOT included in the storyboards?

    a. drawings   **b.** movements   **c.** the script

2. Who is responsible for animating the movements of a cut?

    a. the key animator   **b.** the in-between animator   **c.** the action animator

3. What is one thing that the effects department adds?

    a. shading   **b.** sound effects   **c.** music

Guided Summary 15 Audio

本文の語句を使って、次の要約文を完成させましょう。完成したら、音声を聞いて確認しましょう。

The process of making Japanese animation starts with the ⟨1⟩_____. The next step is ⟨2⟩_____, starting with ⟨3⟩_____—a series of pictures showing what will happen. After that, ⟨4⟩_____ for the scenery and landscape are drawn, and then images are ⟨5⟩_____ produced. Next, it goes to the key animators, and then it's on to the ⟨6⟩_____ _____ animators, who make the cuts look smoother and more ⟨7⟩_____. Next is ⟨8⟩_____ for shading and coloring. The final stage of production is ⟨9⟩_____, where visual images such as smoke are added. Lastly is ⟨10⟩_____, including voice-overs, sound effects, music and final editing.

Writing Strategy

時を表す表現

(1) 前置詞として用いられるもの（at, on, in, during, by など）

at は時間の一点、on は特定の日、in は月や年、during は特定の期間、by は期限を表します。

- The cafe closes **at** midnight.
- The fall semester starts **on** September 20.
- Can you finish the report **by** next Monday?

(2) 接続詞として用いられるもの（when, while, once など）

- Please keep an eye on my dog **while** I am away.
- **Once** the date has been fixed, we will let you know.

(3) 前置詞・接続詞のいずれでも用いられるもの（before, after, until, since など）

- We should stay here **until** noon. until は前置詞
- We should stay here **until** the rain stops. until は接続詞

Check Your Understanding

（　）の中から適切な語句を選び、○で囲みましょう。

1. You will not be allowed to enter the building (during / while) the construction period.

2. I need to submit the assignment (until / by) tomorrow.

3. Text me (on / when) you arrive at the station.

Sentence Writing

A (　　) 内の指示に従って、次の英文を書き換えてみましょう。

1. Please submit your report no later than Friday. (**by** を用いて)

   _____.

2. Brian fell asleep while the game was being played. (**during** を用いて)

   _____.

3. The restaurant stays open until 11 p.m. (**at** を用いて)

   _____.

4. You may not leave the classroom before your teacher gives you permission.

   (**once** を用いて)

   _____

   _____.

B 自分で自由に考えて次の英文を完成させましょう。

1. The first thing I do when I get to school is _____

   _____.

2. I usually _____

   _____ after my last class of the week.

3. We're allowed to _____ and _____

   _____ during class, but we're not permitted to _____

   _____ or _____.

Paragraph Writing

A 次の英文を並べ替えて、１つのパラグラフができるように、適切な番号を下の欄に書いてみましょう。書いたら、音声を聞いて確認しましょう。

1. They are formed when warm, wet air is forced upward by heavier, cool air.

2. These high winds then move in a circular pattern around the eye of the typhoon, where the winds stop and the clouds lift, but the ocean below remains violent.

3. The air pressure subsequently drops quickly from the outer edge towards the center, causing the wind velocity to rise.

4. Typhoons are high-speed windstorms that originate over the ocean, with winds of up to 250 kilometers per hour.

B あなたが作れる簡単な料理（チーズオムレツ、パンケーキなど）について、材料と必要な分量（小麦粉 1/2 カップ、卵 2 個など）をリストし、調理の手順を書きましょう。

Recipe for: _____

Preparation time

Ingredients

Preparation First, _____

　　　　　　　　 Next, _____

　　　　　　　　 _____

　　　　　　　　 _____

　　　　　　　　 Finally, _____

　　　　　　　　 _____

Feeling Through Your Senses

　レオナルド・ダ・ヴィンチの『モナ・リザ』は、世界で最も有名な絵画と言われています。16 世紀初頭に描かれたと考えられているこの作品は、現在でもなお人々を魅了し続けています。この Unit では、数々の画期的な技巧を駆使して描かれた『モナ・リザ』の魅力についての文章を読み、表現に奥行きを与える形容詞や副詞を身につけましょう。

Warm-Up Questions

次の左側にある芸術家の有名な作品を右側から選び、線で結びましょう。

Claude Monet　・	・ *David*
Edvard Munch　・	・ *Guernica*
Leonardo da Vinci　・	・ *Mona Lisa*
Michelangelo　・	・ *Sunflowers*
Pablo Picasso　・	・ *The Scream*
Vincent van Gogh　・	・ *Water Lilies*

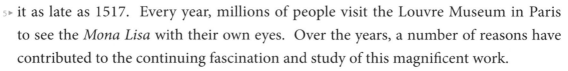

The *Mona Lisa* Continues to Fascinate People

1   Leonardo da Vinci's *Mona Lisa* is probably the most famous painting in the world. It is believed to have been painted between 1503 and 1506 in Florence, Italy, although Leonardo may have continued working on
5▶ it as late as 1517. Every year, millions of people visit the Louvre Museum in Paris to see the *Mona Lisa* with their own eyes. Over the years, a number of reasons have contributed to the continuing fascination and study of this magnificent work.

2   The painting is a half-body portrait of a young woman with a distant landscape in the background. The woman is sitting upright and sideways in a chair, with her
10▶ face and body slightly turned towards the viewer. This three-quarter view quickly became the standard for all portraits, one that is still used today.

3   The delicately painted veil, the finely created long black hair and the carefully crafted folded fabric show Leonardo's great patience and attention to detail. The use of fine shading in the curves of the woman's hair and clothing is repeated in the
15▶ shapes of the valleys and rivers in the background. This synthesis of model and landscape set the norm for all future portraits.

4   Leonardo was fascinated by the way light falls on curved surfaces. He created her veil, hair and skin with ultra-thin layers of transparent color. Her face appears to glow, giving the painting an almost magical quality. But probably the most magical,
20▶ and mysterious, quality of all is her smile. Leonardo created this smile through perspective and by using unique shadow work. The *Mona Lisa*'s famous smile represents the idea of happiness. The smile changes, depending on where the viewer looks. It actually appears more impressive when looking at the portrait's eyes than when looking at the mouth itself.

Notes   sit upright 背筋を伸ばして座る   sideways 横向きに   crafted 作り上げられた   synthesis 統合
transparent color 透過色   perspective 遠近法

Comprehension Questions

本文の内容に関して、次の質問の答えとして適当なものを選びましょう。

1. For what kind of portrait did Leonardo set the standard?

    a. the half-body portrait   **b.** the seated model   **c.** the three-quarter view

2. What did Leonardo use when painting both the model and the landscape?

    a. fine shading   **b.** long brush strokes   **c.** light colors

3. What should viewers look at for the portrait's smile to look the most impressive?

    a. the mouth   **b.** the nose   **c.** the eyes

Guided Summary

 18 Audio

本文の語句を使って、次の要約文を完成させましょう。完成したら、音声を聞いて確認しましょう。

The *Mona Lisa* is a _____[1]_____ portrait of a young woman painted by Leonardo da Vinci between 1503 and 1506. The woman is seated upright and _____[2]_____, her face and body turned slightly towards the viewer. Leonardo's great attention to detail is shown in the _____[3]_____ painted veil, the model's long black hair and the carefully folded _____[4]_____ of her dress. He used fine _____[5]_____ for both the model and the landscape, and ultra-thin layers of _____[6]_____ color. _____[7]_____ and unique _____[8]_____ work are responsible for her famous _____[9]_____, which appears most impressive when looking at the portrait's _____[10]_____.

Writing Strategy

形容詞の働き

(1) 補語になる

- The painting is **famous**. — famous は主格補語
- The song made her **famous**. — famous は目的格補語

(2) 名詞を修飾する

- This is a very **interesting** book. — interesting は book を修飾

副詞の働き

副詞は、動詞・形容詞・他の副詞・文全体を修飾します。

- He **carefully** read the manuscript.

  carefully は read を修飾

- The city looks **completely** different now.

  completely は different を修飾

- The incident happened **quite** recently.

  quite は recently を修飾

- **Surprisingly**, Joe got promoted again.

  surprisingly は文全体を修飾

Check Your Understanding

(　) の中から適切な語句を選び、○で囲みましょう。

1. Good medicine tastes (bitter / bitterly).

2. (Almost / Most) people can't afford to live in this area.

3. I think his English is (such / pretty) good.

4. George works (much / very) harder than anyone else on the team.

5. Bill complains that his salary is (cheap / low).

Sentence Writing

A (　　) 内の指示に従って、次の英文を書き換えてみましょう。

1. Bill speaks eloquently. (**Bill is** で始めて)

_____

2. He insists on his innocence. (**He insists that** で始めて)

_____

3. I was informed that he had arrived there safely. (**I was informed of** で始めて)

_____

_____

4. We are very surprised at his sudden dismissal. (**We are very surprised that** で始めて)

_____

_____

B 次の語句を並び換えて、英文を完成させましょう。

1. rings / busy / the / on / constantly / especially / days, / telephone

_____

_____ in the main office.

2. back / child / noisily / a / row / cried / the / in / small

_____

_____ of the airplane.

3. all / Donald / shocked / were / that / quit / we / to / suddenly / learn

_____

_____ his job.

Paragraph Writing

A 次の英文を並べ替えて、１つのパラグラフができるように、適切な番号を下の欄に書いてみましょう。書いたら、音声を聞いて確認しましょう。

1. The Angkor Wat temple complex is located in the northern province of Siem Reap in Cambodia, and covers an area of approximately 400 square kilometers.

2. In the Khmer Empire, the complex had a high level of social order and ranking, and possessed strong symbolic importance.

3. Therefore, Angkor Wat has both strong cultural, religious and symbolic value, and aesthetic and artistic significance.

4. Located within this large area are numerous magnificent temples exemplary of Khmer architecture, as well as basins, reservoirs, canals and communication routes.

Note: Khmer Empire クメール帝国

B 自分の好きな場所（カフェ、美術館、公園、海など）を１つ選び、できるだけ多くの形容詞と副詞を用いて詳細に記述してみましょう。

One of my favorite places is _____

_____

_____

_____

_____

_____

_____

_____

_____

_____

Don't You Agree?

　みなさんは、勉強中に音楽を聴くことはありますか。音楽が様々な心理効果を引き起こすことは、多数の研究で報告されています。では、音楽を聴くことは勉強に良い作用をもたらすのでしょうか。この Unit では、勉強中に聴く音楽がもたらしうる効果について述べた文章を読み、英語で説得力のある文章を書くための表現方法を身につけましょう。

Warm-Up Questions

次の質問に対して適当な答えを選び、☑をつけましょう。2つ以上つけることもできます。2. の質問ではその理由も英語で書きましょう。

1. Where do you sometimes study?

☐ Bedroom　　　☐ Living room　　　☐ Library

☐ Train　　　☐ Café　　　☐ Other: _____

2. Do you listen to music when you study?

☐ Yes, because _____.

☐ No, because _____.

Listening to Music While Studying Can Make You a Better Student

1 Music is a powerful art form that can affect our emotions, inspire us and alter our mood. And while most students listen to music while studying simply because they like music and/or it makes the process less painful, studies suggest that
5▶ it can also make us better and smarter students.

2 Music has the ability to give us great pleasure. It induces pleasurable emotions and triggers the release of a chemical in our brains that causes feelings of happiness and excitement. Listening to music also lowers cortisol levels. Cortisol is often called the "stress hormone" because of its connection to the stress response. Research
10▶ shows that we are generally better at solving problems when we are in a positive or happy mood as opposed to a negative or neutral mood. For study sessions that last for more than an hour at a time, background music helps us maintain our focus and motivation for longer periods of time.

3 It is true that listening to music with lyrics can be quite distracting while we
15▶ are trying to study. Our brain struggles to process the lyrics and focus on our schoolwork at the same time. However, a number of studies have found that listening to soothing music without lyrics may help us study better. Many researchers believe that this type of music puts students at ease and makes them more receptive learners.

4 In summary, if you ever need to find a way to stay focused or to concentrate
20▶ while studying, then why not try listening to classical music or some other form of soothing instrumental music during your study sessions? It may relax you and put you in a pleasant mood, and thereby enable you to learn more quickly and easily, as well as make you a better student.

Notes　induce 引き起こす　trigger 誘発する　cortisol コルチゾール　lyrics 歌詞　soothing 気持ちを落ち着かせる
receptive 受容力がある、理解が早い

46

Comprehension Questions

本文の内容に関して、次の質問の答えとして適当なものを選びましょう。

1. What does NOT increase as result of listening to music?

   a. cortisol production 　　**b.** problem solving ability 　　**c.** pleasurable emotions

2. For longer study sessions, what does background music help people do?

   a. stay focused 　　**b.** maintain a neutral mood 　　**c.** process lyrics

3. What kind of music does the author suggest students listen to while studying?

   a. soothing music with lyrics 　　**b.** opera music 　　　　**c.** instrumental music

Guided Summary 21 Audio

本文の語句を（適切な形に直して）使って、次の要約文を完成させましょう。完成したら、音声を聞いて確認しましょう。

Many students like listening to music while studying, and studies indicate that it can also make them better and _____1_____ students. Music induces pleasurable _____2_____. It causes the release of a _____3_____ in the _____4_____ that makes us feel happy and excited. Music also _____5_____ the level of a "stress hormone" called _____6_____, and people are better at _____7_____ problems when they're in a happy or positive mood. Background music also helps people stay focused and _____8_____ for longer periods of time. Researchers have found that soothing _____9_____ music works best to put students at ease and make them more _____10_____ learners.

Writing Strategy

無生物主語

英語では、原因・理由、手段、条件となるものを主語として、「それが人を〜する（させる）」という形式がよく用いられます。

- **This app** enables you to get relevant information immediately.

  = Thanks to this app, you can get relevant information immediately.

- **These CDs** made me feel nostalgic.

  = When I listened to these CDs, I felt nostalgic.

- **What** made him think that way?

  = Why did he think that way?

- **This train** will take you to the airport.

  = If you take this train, you will get to the airport.

- **The experience** caused him to consider his future.

  = Because of the experience, he considered his future.

Check Your Understanding

下の囲みの中の語句から適切なものを選んで、次の英文を完成させましょう。

remind	prevented	make	show

1. The landslides (   ) us from driving to the village.

2. This medicine will (   ) you feel better.

3. These pictures (   ) me of my father.

4. This DVD will (   ) you how to lose weight in 10 days.

Sentence Writing

A (　　) 内の指示に従って、次の英文を書き換えてみましょう。

1. Thanks to the Internet, we can share ideas with everyone in the world.

(**enable** を用いて)

_____

_____

2. If you read this brochure, you will get an idea of what it's like to work here.

(**give** を用いて)

_____

_____

3. After a two-hour drive from LA, we arrived at the valley. (**bring** を用いて)

_____

4. Because of the heavy rain, the river overflowed its banks. (**cause** を用いて)

_____

B 無生物主語を含むように、自分で自由に考えて次の英文を完成させましょう。

1. Smartphones allow _____

_____ .

2. _____ makes me sleepy.

3. Eating a well-balanced diet and exercising regularly will _____

_____ . In contrast, smoking every day

_____ .

4. _____ makes me feel as if

_____ .

Paragraph Writing

A 次の英文を並び替えて、1つのパラグラフができるように、適切な番号を下の欄に書いてみましょう。書いたら、音声を聞いて確認しましょう。

22
Audio

1. Removing the need to drive by offering home visits by doctors and food delivery services will also help because it will mean fewer elderly people on the road.

2. Just as mandatory seat belt usage and air bags have reduced traffic fatalities, it's reasonable to think that such additional safety features will have a similar effect.

3. In order to address this problem, the government needs to promote vehicles with advanced safety technology such as automatic braking systems.

4. In Japan, drivers aged 75 or older cause fatal accidents at a much higher rate than younger drivers.

B 自由な時間 (free time) とお金 (money) はどちらがより大切だと思いますか。自分の意見を論証してみましょう。

In my view, _____ is more important than _____. _____

You Be the Judge

　ファッションブランドというと、かつてはもっぱら高級ブランドを連想させましたが、今では手頃な価格の衣料ブランドも人気です。ユニクロは、良質の衣料を低価格で提供するファッションブランドとして今日まで成長し続けてきました。この Unit では、ユニクロの成功要因についての文章を読み、批評や評価を表現するための練習をしましょう。

Warm-Up Questions

次の質問に対して **1.** では英語で答え、**2.** では適当な答えを選び、☑ をつけましょう。2つ以上つけることもできます。

1. Where do you like to shop for clothes? _____

2. What's your image of UNIQLO?

   ☐ Inexpensive ☐ Simple ☐ Good quality ☐ Global

   ☐ Fashionable ☐ HeatTech ☐ TV commercials

   ☐ Other: _____

UNIQLO—Four Strategies for Success

1　Japanese fashion brand UNIQLO has successfully established a unique position in the apparel industry by focusing on well-made basics and its corporate values rather than on the most recent fashion trends.　Its business strategy focuses on innovation, a "made for all" philosophy, product offerings and social responsibility.
5▶ A closer evaluation of these elements will tell us why UNIQLO has grown to become the third largest apparel retailer in the world, behind only ZARA and H&M.

2　**Innovation**　UNIQLO's reputation as a technology-driven clothing brand is well deserved.　Its apparel offers unique functional performance, thanks to its design innovation, none greater than its HeatTech products.　Annual sales of its HeatTech
10▶ products have grown from 1.5 million items in 2003 to well over 100 million today.

3　**"Made for All"**　UNIQLO's brand philosophy is "Made for All."　It does not define its target customers in terms of gender, age, or ethnicity.　It targets all people. Apparel makers often focus on specific designs to satisfy their target customers, but UNIQLO serves a wide range of customers by offering high-quality casual wear at
15▶ low prices.

4　**Product Offerings**　UNIQLO carries a moderate selection of casual basics which can be easily coordinated with other items.　Rather than overwhelming consumers by constantly restocking its shelves with trendy fashion items, UNIQLO offers a carefully considered selection of "seasonless," essential products.　This strategy has
20▶ proven successful, as customers of all ages like to wear basic designs.

5　**Social Responsibility**　Surveys consistently indicate that customers expect companies to be good corporate citizens.　UNIQLO believes that a company's value is closely linked to the value it brings to society as a whole, and that successful companies have a duty to serve society.　Its Factory Worker Empowerment Project
25▶ (FWEP), which helps women in Bangladesh and Indonesia to acquire basic living skills, is just one example of UNIQLO's commitment to social responsibility.

Notes　▶　ethnicity 民族性　overwhelm 圧倒する　restock 補充する　corporate citizen 企業市民　commitment 献身

Comprehension Questions

本文の内容に関して、次の質問の答えとして適当なものを選びましょう。

1. What are UNIQLO's HeatTech products an example of?

    a. brand philosophy   **b.** functional performance   **c.** social responsibility

2. What is UNIQLO's target market?

    a. teenagers and young adults   **b.** mainly women   **c.** all people

3. What words best describe UNIQLO's products?

    a. casual and basic   **b.** lightweight and affordable   **c.** trendy and fashionable

Guided Summary

24 Audio

本文の語句を使って、次の要約文を完成させましょう。完成したら、音声を聞いて確認しましょう。

UNIQLO has become the world's third largest apparel ___1___ by
focusing on well-made basics, in contrast to other major fashion brands. The
company's business ___2___ centers around innovation, a "made
for all" ___3___, product offerings and social responsibility.
Thanks to its design ___4___ including its HeatTech products,
UNIQLO's apparel provides unique ___5___ performance.
It has a wide target market, and it offers a ___6___ selection
of items that are easy to ___7___ with other items. The
company is committed to being a good corporate ___8___. It believes
that a company's value is closely ___9___ with the value it brings to
___10___ as a whole.

Writing Strategy

(1) 現在完了

< have/has + 過去分詞 > の形で、動作や出来事が現在までに完了したこと、現在までの経験、状態の継続などを表します。明確な過去の一時点を表す表現（yesterdayや～ days ago など）がある場合は、現在完了は使えません。

- I **haven't finished** the assignment. — 完了

- Lucy **has gone** to Paris. — 結果

- **Have** you ever **been** to Paris? — 経験

- We **have known** each other since childhood. — 継続

(2) 過去完了

< had + 過去分詞 > の形で、過去のある時点までの動作や状態の「完了」「結果」「経験」「継続」などを表します。

- Japan **had become** the second largest economy by the mid-1970s. — 完了

- I **had met** her several times before then. — 経験

また、2つの過去の出来事を描写する場合、時間上の前後関係を示すために、先に起こった出来事を< had +過去分詞 >で表すことがあります。

- The meeting ended much earlier than I **had expected**.

Check Your Understanding

（　）の中から適切な語句を選び、○で囲みましょう。

1. Until then we (never hear / had never heard) of the disease.

2. I (have been / had been) living alone since I was 18.

3. I (bought / have bought) the camera two days ago.

Sentence Writing

A ( ) 内の指示に従って、次の英文を書き換えてみましょう。

1. Jason went to England. He is not here now. (現在完了を用いて1つの文に)

_____

2. Mary started practicing the piano when she was five. She is still practicing it.

(現在完了進行形を用いて1つの文に)

_____

_____

3. It's almost five years since we moved to this city. (**Almost five years** で始めて)

_____

_____

4. Dustin first saw a raccoon when he went to North Carolina.

(**Dustin had never** で始めて)

_____

_____

B ( ) 内の語句を使って、適切な完了時制にして、次の英文を完成させましょう。 **3.** は適当な過去分詞を自分で自由に考えて書きましょう。

1. I'm not hungry. _____ . (**already, eat**)

2. By the time I went to bed last night, _____
my homework.

(**already, finish**)

3. I have already _____ and _____

_____ today, but I haven't _____ or

_____ yet.

Paragraph Writing

A 次の英文を並べ替えて、1つのパラグラフができるように、適切な番号を下の欄に書いてみましょう。書いたら、音声を聞いて確認しましょう。

25
Audio

1. Squash also improves hand-eye coordination, as players repeatedly have to see and follow the ball while adjusting their bodies and hands to make contact with it.

2. Squash is consistently ranked at the top of the list of healthiest sports.

3. In addition to its physical benefits, squash also ensures mental well-being, as it becomes more of a mental sport than a physical sport once players build up their endurance.

4. This is based on factors including cardio and muscular endurance, possible injury risks, and calories burned during a 30-minute session.

B あなたが最近行った飲食店について、以下の基準と評語をもとに批評を書いてみましょう。

> **Criteria:** 1) food quality   2) service   3) atmosphere   4) price
>
> **Rating:** excellent   very good   good   satisfactory   poor

I recently ate at _____. I ordered _____.

The food quality was _____

_____. The service was _____ and the servers were _____

_____. The atmosphere was _____.

There was _____.

The price _____. My meal cost ¥_____.

Two Sides to Every Story

　医学研究や新薬開発の多くは、動物実験によって支えられています。動物実験は、動物の尊い犠牲を伴うため、その是非をめぐる議論は昔から絶えません。医科学の発展にとって動物実験はやむを得ないという意見がある一方で、人道的観点から動物実験に反対する意見もあります。この Unit では、動物実験の賛成論と反対論について読み、議論を展開するための英語表現を学びましょう。

Warm-Up Questions

次の質問に対して、**1.** では英語で答え、**2.** では適当な答えを選び、☑をつけて、その理由を英語で書きましょう。

1. What are some things that animals provide us with? (for example, milk)

_____ / _____ / _____ / _____

2. Do you think it's OK to use animals for experiments?

　　☐ Yes, because _____.

　　☐ No, because _____.

The Debate over Animal Testing

1   Every year, millions of animals are used for developing and checking the effectiveness and safety of medicines to treat and prevent diseases and other medical conditions in humans. Although the practice has continued for centuries, the question of whether animals should be used in experiments remains hotly debated
5▶ today. Let's look at some of the pros and cons of animal testing.

2   On the one hand, those in favor of animal testing argue that it has resulted in the development of countless life-saving medicines for not only humans but also animals. The California Biomedical Research Association says that nearly every medical breakthrough in the last hundred years was made possible by animal testing. For
10▶ example, the polio vaccine, first tested on animals, reduced the number of polio cases from 350,000 in 1988 to just 27 in 2016. People who support animal experiments also say that, thanks to strict regulations, there is no mistreatment of laboratory animals.

3   On the other hand, opponents of animal testing say that it is cruel and inhumane
15▶ to use animals for experimental purposes. They claim that lab animals suffer both physical pain and psychological suffering, and that many of them are killed after the experiments are completed. Opponents also argue that there are alternative methods that can be used instead of animal testing, and because animals are so different from humans, animal tests do not correctly predict real-world human reactions.
20▶ Furthermore, they say that drugs that pass animal tests are not necessarily safe when used on humans.

4   The cases for and against experiments on animals are both strong, and reflect the thoughts of two groups having completely different ways of thinking—one which points to the benefits that animal testing can bring to humans, the other to the cruelty
25▶ and unethical treatment of the animals that are tested.

Notes   pros and cons 賛否   breakthrough 大発見、画期的進歩   polio vaccine ポリオワクチン   mistreatment 虐待
inhumane 非人道的な   unethical 非倫理的な

Comprehension Questions

本文の内容に関して、次の質問の答えとして適当なものを選びましょう。

1. What view does the passage take on the subject of animal testing?

   a. It should be allowed.   **b.** It shouldn't be allowed.

   c. It is neutral on the subject.

2. What does the California Biomedical Research Association say that animal testing is responsible for?

   a. most medical advances   **b.** stronger medicines   **c.** better animal treatment

3. What is one argument made by opponents of animal testing?

   a. It's too expensive.   **b.** It causes pain and suffering.   **c.** It's outdated.

Guided Summary

本文の語句を使って、次の要約文を完成させましょう。完成したら、音声を聞いて確認しましょう。

There's a heated debate as to whether ___1___ testing should be
used to develop and check the ___2___ and safety of
medicines in order to treat and ___3___ diseases in humans. Those
in favor point out that countless ___4___ have been saved as a result of
animal testing, and that most ___5___ breakthroughs have resulted
from such testing. ___6___ maintain that animal experiments
are cruel and ___7___, and that results from experiments on
animals can be dangerous when applied to ___8___. The cases
for and against animal testing are both ___9___ and represent two
different ways of ___10___.

59

Writing Strategy

相関接続詞

　前後 2 つの要素が組になって使われる接続詞を相関接続詞といいます。相関接続詞が主語の位置にある場合、both A and B は複数扱い、A as well as B は原則として A の数に動詞を一致させ、それ以外は原則として動詞に近い方に一致させます。

- **Both** Mary **and** Ann speak English.

- **Not only** you **but also** I am responsible for it.

- **Either** you **or** Margaret is wrong.

- John **as well as** his friends was involved in the accident.

群前置詞

　2 つ以上の語が結合して 1 つの前置詞として働くものを群前置詞といいます。

according to 〜（〜によると）、due to 〜（〜が原因で）、instead of 〜（〜の代わりに、〜しないで）、in addition to 〜（〜に加えて）、in case of 〜（〜の場合には）、in favor of 〜（〜に賛成して、〜の利益となるように）、in spite of 〜（〜にもかかわらず）、in terms of 〜（〜に関して、〜の点から）、regardless of 〜（〜にかかわらず）、thanks to 〜（〜のおかげで）などがあります。

- **In case of** fire, sound the alarm.

- This car is better than that one **in terms of** fuel efficiency.

- I'm getting better **thanks to** the medicine.

Check Your Understanding

（　）の中から適切な語句を選び、○で囲みましょう。

1. (Either / Both) you or I was supposed to arrange a flight for them.

2. (In spite of / Despite of) his efforts, he wasn't able to pass the exam.

3. You should walk to work (instead of / thanks to) going by car.

Sentence Writing

A ( ) 内の指示に従って、次の英文を書き換えてみましょう。

1. The weather forecast says that it's going to rain tomorrow. (**according to** を用いて)

_____

_____

2. In addition to being a philosopher, he is a great poet. (**not only** … **but also** を用いて)

_____

3. Although he was popular, he didn't win the presidential election.

(**in spite of** を用いて)

_____

_____

4. All new members are welcome no matter how old they are. (**regardless of** を用いて)

_____

_____

B 自分で自由に考えて次の英文を完成させましょう。

1. In terms of music, I like both _____

and _____.

2. Thanks to my parents, _____

_____.

3. According to today's news report, _____

_____.

4. In addition to being _____, my best friend is also

_____ and _____.

Paragraph Writing

A 次の英文を並べ替えて、1つのパラグラフができるように、適切な番号を下の欄に書いてみましょう。書いたら、音声を聞いて確認しましょう。

1. Working part-time also teaches students valuable life skills such as time management, interpersonal communication and networking.

2. On the downside, however, working too many hours can lead to sleep deprivation and other health issues, as well as poor grades in school.

3. There are many things to consider before making the decision to get a job while studying in university.

4. Most students, of course, work for the money, whether it be to pay for rent and food, or simply to earn some extra money for their own pleasure.

B ネットショッピングの長所と短所をそれぞれ何点か考え、以下のパラグラフを完成させましょう。

Nowadays, there are thousands of online shopping sites, selling just about everything you can possibly imagine. Online shopping, however, has both advantages and disadvantages. One of the biggest advantages of online shopping is _____

_____

_____

_____

_____

_____

_____

10 A Bit of Advice

　大学生にとって、就職活動が精神的にも肉体的にも大きな負担となることはまれではありません。中でも面接は特に緊張を伴うものです。面接官に対して良い印象を与えるには、どのような準備をしておくべきなのでしょうか。この Unit では、就職活動での面接のアドバイスを述べた文章を読み、英語で助言を与える文章を書く際に役立つ表現を学びましょう。

Warm-Up Questions

次の質問に対して **1.** では英語で答え、**2.** では重要度を①〜③から選び、番号を空欄に書きましょう。

1. What kind of job would you like to have after you graduate?

_____

2. What's important to you when choosing a job?

| ① Very important |
| ② Somewhat important |
| ③ Not very important |

(　　) Location 　　　　　　(　　) Salary

(　　) Size of the company 　(　　) Commuting time

(　　) Enjoyment 　　　　　(　　) Working hours

(　　) Other: _____

Resume

Keys to a Successful Job Interview

1　A job interview can be one of the most stressful experiences you'll ever have, especially the first one. Let's assume that you've found the right job for you, sent off your résumé and cover letter, and have been invited for an interview. What should you expect? While it's impossible to predict exactly what you will be
5▶ asked, many Japanese companies take a rather formulaic approach. It would be in your best interest to become familiar with this approach.

2　First, you will likely be asked to introduce yourself. It's a good idea to keep your answer fairly short and to the point, without getting into too much detail. In addition, you will almost certainly be asked why you want to work for the company.
10▶ It's very important that you prepare carefully for this question in advance. Your answer represents an opportunity to make a strong impression on the interviewers by demonstrating your in-depth knowledge of the company and stating clearly why the company best fits your qualifications, skills and long-term goals. You should also be prepared to discuss your strengths and weaknesses. You're advised to emphasize your
15▶ strengths without sounding overconfident. If you're asked about your weaknesses, mention one that isn't relevant to the position. For example, admitting that you're not a good public speaker probably won't hurt your chances of being hired as a software engineer.

3　At the end of the interview, you may be asked if you have any questions. It's
20▶ a good idea to prepare some questions in advance in case this opportunity arises. Questions such as career advancement opportunities and working hours are appropriate questions. Finally, end the interview in a polite manner by standing, stating that it was an honor meeting everyone, and bowing. If all goes well, you'll hear from them again soon. Good luck!

Notes　résumé 履歴書　predict 予測する　formulaic 型通りの　qualification 資格、資質　emphasize 強調する
overconfident 自信過剰な　relevant 関連性のある

Comprehension Questions

本文の内容に関して、次の質問の答えとして適当なものを選びましょう。

1. How might job interviews in Japan be described?

   a. short and to the point　　b. similar in their approach　　c. very hard to predict

2. What will likely make a strong impression on interviewers?

   a. a detailed self-introduction　　b. a neat appearance
   c. knowledge of the company

3. What should job interviewees do if they are asked to describe their weaknesses?

   a. mention one that is not related to the job
   b. point out a few minor weaknesses　　c. say they don't have any weaknesses

Guided Summary

本文の語句を（適切な形に直して）使って、次の要約文を完成させましょう。完成したら、音声を聞いて確認しましょう。

For a successful job ___1___ in Japan, it's important to prepare for some questions that you'll likely be asked. First, you should come prepared to ___2___ yourself briefly and to explain ___3___ you want to work for the company. Demonstrate your ___4___ of the company, and why the company fits your ___5___, skills and future ___6___. Be ready to discuss your strengths and ___7___, but mention only one unimportant weak point.

Also, be prepared to ___8___ a few well-thought-out questions of your own.

After the interview, you should stand up, tell your interviewers that you were ___9___ to meet them, and ___10___.

Writing Strategy

形式主語（仮主語）

　本来の主語の代わりに、形式上の主語として用いられる it のことを形式主語（仮主語）といいます。形式主語が用いられる場合、内容を持った本来の主語（真主語）は後ろに置かれます。形式主語は、to 不定詞や that 節が主語になる場合によく用いられます。

(1) <It is 形容詞 (for X) to ... > の形式をとれる形容詞
　　（easy, difficult, hard, dangerous, useful など）

- **It** is hard **to** tell the difference between them.

- **It** is quite easy for me **to** solve the problem.

(2) <It is 形容詞 that ... > の形式をとれる形容詞
　　（certain, clear, obvious, true など）

- **It** is clear **that** both of them are mistaken.

- **It** is true **that** the company went bankrupt.

(3) (1) と (2) のいずれの形式もとれる形容詞（important, strange, natural, necessary など）

- **It** is natural for you **to** think so.

　= **It** is natural **that** you think so.

- **It** is important for me **to** take the course.

　= **It** is important **that** I take the course.

Check Your Understanding

（　）の中から適切な語句を選び、○で囲みましょう。

1. It would be easy (that you / for you to) pass the exam.

2. (It / He) is impossible to tell what will happen.

3. It was (glad / fortunate) that he was there to help her.

Sentence Writing

A (   ) 内の指示に従って、次の英文を書き換えてみましょう。

1. We cannot deny that he saved us. (**It is impossible** で始めて)

   _____

2. Not surprisingly, Bruce was opposed to the plan. (**It is not surprising** で始めて)

   _____

   _____

3. More than 20 people are reported to have been injured in the accident.

   (**It is reported** で始めて)

   _____

   _____

4. You were careless to leave your passport in the taxi. (**It was careless** で始めて)

   _____

   _____

B 自分で自由に考えて次の英文を完成させましょう。

1. It's difficult for me to _____

   _____.

2. In Japan, it's common to _____

   _____.

3. I think it's important for people to _____

   _____.

4. It's disappointing that _____

   _____.

Paragraph Writing

A 次の英文を並べ替えて、１つのパラグラフができるように、適切な番号を下の欄に書いてみましょう。書いたら、音声を聞いて確認しましょう。

1. Some students enter university knowing exactly what they want to do after graduating, and successfully find employment in their chosen field.

2. The main thing is not to let your indecision bring you down or to accept a job offer for work that you have no particular interest in.

3. However, if you are like most students and are uncertain about what career path to follow, you shouldn't worry. In the words of Michael Jackson, "You are not alone."

4. Instead, why don't you think of it as a positive thing and use it to your advantage by exploring different career options that you never considered before?

B あなたの大学に入学したいと考えている人に送るアドバイスを考え、以下のパラグラフを完成させましょう。

For anyone planning on entering this university next year, let me offer you three pieces of advice. First, _____

_____

_____

_____

_____

_____

_____

_____

_____

Please Don't Misunderstand

テレビゲームの暴力的なシーンが人の人格や行動に悪影響を与えるのではないかという懸念の声は巷でよく聞かれます。実際に、暴力的なテレビゲームで遊ぶことによって、攻撃的な行動が多くなることはあるのでしょうか。この Unit では、テレビゲームと実際の行動の関係性について述べた文章を読み、物事の説明を明確化するのに役立つ英語表現を身につけましょう。

Warm-Up Questions

次の質問に対して、**1.** では英語で答え、**2.** では適当な答えを選び、☑および◎をつけましょう。

1. How often do you play video games? (every day, once a week, etc.)

_____

2. What kind of video games do you like? ☑
What's your favorite kind? (◎)

☐ ( ) Role playing ☐ ( ) Shooting ☐ ( ) Action ☐ ( ) Trading card game

☐ ( ) Adventure ☐ ( ) Simulation ☐ ( ) Other: _____

Violent Video Games and Real-Life Violence

1   There is a video game called *Fortnite* in which
up to 100 players parachute onto a small island,
search for armor and weapons, and then kill or hide from
other players in an attempt to be the lone survivor. The game has attracted millions
5► of players around the world. The popularity of these types of games raises questions
about whether there is a direct link between violent gaming and a person's behavior.
In other words, do violent video games lead to real-life violence?

2   Studies have shown that playing violent video games can increase aggressive
behaviors. Violent video games can also make people less sensitive and feel less
10► empathy when they see violent behavior. However, this does not mean that violent
video games necessarily result in real-life violence, or that they affect everyone in the
same way. And while it is true that violence is a form of aggression, not all aggressive
behaviors are violent. Very few studies have specifically examined whether playing
violent video games increases the chances of violent acts.

15► **3**   The general perception that playing violent video games leads to real-life violence
is likely affected by publication bias. Studies pointing to such a link are more likely to
be published than studies having contrary conclusions. In fact, there is a large body
of research that has found no link at all. Many criminologists have come to the same
conclusion.

20► **4**   To sum up, there is no conclusive evidence suggesting that playing violent video
games leads to violent behavior. This is not to say that a connection doesn't exist, but
rather that we simply don't know for sure. It's important to keep in mind that violent
video game exposure is one risk factor of aggressive behavior, which may or may not
lead to acts of real-life violence.

Notes   armor 鎧   lone 唯一の   aggressive 攻撃的な   empathy 共感、感情移入   publication bias 出版バイアス
criminologist 犯罪学者   risk factor 危険因子

Comprehension Questions

本文の内容に関して、次の質問の答えとして適当なものを選びましょう。

1. How may violent video games make people feel when they see violent behavior?

   a. more inactive   **b.** more insensitive   **c.** more independent

2. What is true of aggressive behavior?

   a. It is always violent.   **b.** It starts from playing violent video games.
   c. It may or may not be linked to violence.

3. According to the passage, do violent video games lead to real-life violence?

   a. Yes, in most cases.   **b.** No, there is no connection.   **c.** It's not known for sure.

Guided Summary

33
Audio

本文の語句を使って、次の要約文を完成させましょう。完成したら、音声を聞いて確認しましょう。

Some studies have found that playing violent video games can increase aggressive ____1____ and reduce people's sensitivity and feelings of ____2____ when they see violent actions. However, not all aggressive behaviors are ____3____ acts, and people don't react to violence in video games in the same ____4____. Furthermore, the general ____5____ that there is a direct link between violent games and a person's behavior is likely affected by publication ____6____. In fact, many researchers, as well as ____7____, have found no ____8____ between the two. In short, there is no conclusive ____9____ which proves that violent video games ____10____ to real-life violence.

71

Writing Strategy

英語には様々な品詞の否定を表す語句があります。

(1) 副詞として働く否定表現（not, never, hardly, rarely など）

- The client **never** shows up on time.

(2) 形容詞として働く否定表現
（no, few, little など）

- There are **few** mistakes in your report.

(3) 代名詞として働く否定表現
（nothing, no one, nobody, none など）

- **Nobody** was in the room when the earthquake happened.

(4) 否定の意味を持つ慣用表現（far from, the last 〜 , anything but など）

- Andrew would be **the last** person to say such a thing.

部分否定

否定表現が「全体」や「完全」などの意味を含む語（all, always, entirely, every, necessarily など）を打ち消すと「（必ずしも / 全てが）〜とは限らない」という部分否定の意味になります。

- The rich are **not necessarily** happier than the poor.

Check Your Understanding

（　　）の中から適切な語句を選び、○で囲みましょう。

1. (Few / Little) people understand the meaning of life.

2. This doesn't (necessary / necessarily) mean that he is a liar.

3. Not (all / every) scholars share the same view.

Sentence Writing

A ( ) 内の指示に従って、次の英文を書き換えてみましょう。

1. Julie is not happy at all. (**far from** を用いて)

_____

2. Jason is least likely to take a bribe. (**the last person** を用いて)

_____

_____

3. Hardly anyone responded to the questionnaire. (**few** を用いて)

_____

_____

4. Everything will be ready soon. (**It won't be** で始めて)

_____

B 自分で自由に考えて次の英文を完成させましょう。

1. Jane is very healthy. She hardly ever _____ , she never

_____ , and she doesn't _____ .

2. In my neighborhood, there are few _____

and no _____ .

3. No one in my family _____ or

_____ .

4. It won't be long before I _____

_____ .

Paragraph Writing

A 次の英文を並べ替えて、１つのパラグラフができるように、適切な番号を下の欄に書いてみましょう。書いたら、音声を聞いて確認しましょう。

1. Conversely, if you buy potato chips in the US, you're getting crisps in the UK.

2. For the most part, Americans and Britons use the same words when talking about food, but be careful, as there are a few exceptions.

3. For Japanese, then, *fried potatoes* and *potato chips* are French fries and potato chips in the US, and chips and crisps in the UK.

4. For example, if you ask for chips in the UK, you'll get what Americans call French fries.

B 日本人に関する以下の３つの固定観念について、誤解を訂正しましょう。

> **Stereotype 1:** Japanese people all love sushi and eat it every day.
> **Stereotype 2:** Japanese people all live in houses with tatami mat floors.
> **Stereotype 3:** Japanese people all watch anime and read manga every day.

While it is true that many Japanese people love sushi, _____

_____

_____

_____

_____

_____

_____

Revisiting the Past

　人類で初めて月面に降り立った宇宙飛行士はニール・アームストロングとバズ・オルドリンですが、彼らを乗せたアポロ11号にはもう1人の宇宙飛行士マイケル・コリンズもいました。アポロ11号が月面に着陸した時、コリンズはどのような任務を果たしたのでしょうか。このUnitでは、個人の追憶や回想、またそれを伝達するための表現方法を学びましょう。

Warm-Up Questions

次の質問に対する適当な答えを選び、☑ をつけましょう。また、**3.** ではその理由を英語で書きましょう。

1. Who was the first person to set foot on the Moon?

☐ Michael Collins ☐ Neil Armstrong ☐ Yuri Gagarin

2. What was the nationality of the first person to journey into outer space?

☐ American ☐ British ☐ French ☐ Russian

3. Would you like to travel into outer space?

☐ Yes, because ＿＿＿＿＿＿＿＿＿＿. ☐ No, because ＿＿＿＿＿＿＿＿＿＿.

Michael Collins Remembers Apollo 11

1   On July 20, 1969, the Apollo 11 lunar module touched down on the Moon. Soon after, two astronauts, Neil Armstrong and Buzz Aldrin, became the first human beings to walk on the
5▸ lunar surface. A third astronaut, Michael Collins, remained in the Apollo command module circling the Moon. Collins was often called "the loneliest man" after he returned to Earth, although he never once felt that way. While his crewmates were busy landing, conducting experiments and collecting Moon samples, Collins was making sure that
10▸ all systems were working properly so that the three of them could return home safely. He recalled that the command module was "a happy home," with hot coffee, music and people to talk to on the radio. He enjoyed his time alone.

2   The Moon was their destination, but for Collins, the most amazing discovery was Earth itself. Fifty years after the lunar landing, Collins had this to say: "The
15▸ Moon was nothing compared to my view of home planet. It was *it*. … I'd look out the window and there would be a tiny little thing, and you could obscure it with your thumb. … It was gorgeous. It was tiny, shiny—the blue of the oceans, the white of the clouds, a little streak of rust color that we call continents. It just glowed."

3   Seeing the Earth from a distance of nearly 400,000 km gave Collins a much
20▸ greater sense of Earth's fragility and a much greater desire to do something to protect that fragility—to protect our planet Earth. Collins may not have enjoyed the glory of setting foot on the Moon for the first time in human history—that belongs to Armstrong and Aldrin—but he was happy with his role, and he felt proud and honored to be a part of that history.

Notes   lunar module 月着陸船   command module （宇宙船の）司令室   crewmate 乗組員仲間
obscure 覆い隠す   streak 筋、線   fragility 脆弱性、もろさ

Comprehension Questions

本文の内容に関して、次の質問の答えとして適当なものを選びましょう。

1. What was Collins responsible for on the Apollo 11 mission?

   a. conducting experiments　　b. maintaining the systems
   c. landing on the Moon

2. What impressed Collins the most about his journey?

   a. the view of Earth　　b. the command module
   c. the beauty of the Moon

3. What did Collins think when he saw Earth from space?

   a. Human beings are fragile.　　b. Time is precious.　　c. Earth is delicate.

Guided Summary

36 Audio

本文の語句を使って、次の要約文を完成させましょう。完成したら、音声を聞いて確認しましょう。

On July 20, 1969, Apollo 11 astronauts Neil Armstrong and Buzz Aldrin became the
first humans to walk on the ____1____ . A third ____2____ ,
Michael Collins, remained aboard the ____3____ module, keeping
all ____4____ running smoothly for the trip back home. The most
amazing ____5____ for Collins was not the Moon, but Earth itself.
He recalled that Earth was gorgeous and that it just " ____6____ ." But
it also looked ____7____ , and he wanted to help ____8____
that fragility. Collins didn't experience the ____9____ of setting foot on the
Moon, but he felt proud and ____10____ to be a part of the historic
mission.

Writing Strategy

他者の言葉を伝える

(1) 直接話法

誰かの発言を第三者に伝える時、発言された言葉をそのまま引用する方法を直接話法といいます。直接話法では、実際に発せられた言葉を引用符で囲み、そのまま引用します。

● John said, "I'm hungry."

> 引用符で囲まれた部分は John の実際の発言

(2) 間接話法

他者の発言を、伝達する人の言葉で言い直した方法を間接話法といいます。間接話法を用いる場合は、主節の動詞の時制に応じて伝達部分の動詞の時制の一致が起こり、代名詞なども伝達者の視点に合わせて変わります。

● John said, "I'm hungry." 　直接話法

　➡ John said (that) he was hungry. 　間接話法

伝達される内容が疑問文の場合、間接話法では主節動詞は ask を用います。また伝達部分は、yes/no 疑問文の場合は接続詞 if（または whether）が導く名詞節、wh 疑問文の場合は疑問詞が導く名詞節に書き換えます。

● John said to me, "Have you read the book?"

　➡ John **asked** me if/whether I had read the book.

● John said to me, "What are you doing?"

　➡ John **asked** me what I was doing.

Check Your Understanding

( ) の中から適切な語句を選び、○で囲みましょう。

1. Katy asked me why (I was / was I) there.

2. James asked them (what / whether) they were discussing.

3. I (told / asked) Bill that I wanted to help him.

Sentence Writing

A (   ) 内の指示に従って、次の英文を書き換えてみましょう。

1. Ken said, "I'm busy now." (**Ken said that** で始めて)

_____

2. Jack said to his mother, "Where are you going?" (間接話法を用いて)

_____

_____

3. Michael said to me, "Are you going to my sister's place?" (間接話法を用いて)

_____

_____

4. Liz said, "Let's take a taxi to the station." (**Liz suggested that** で始めて)

_____

_____

B 自分で自由に考えて次の英文を完成させましょう。

1. Our English teacher told us to _____

_____.

2. Our English teacher told us that _____

_____.

3. Recently, my _____ asked me _____

_____.

4. The other day, I asked _____

what _____.

Paragraph Writing

A 次の英文を並べ替えて、1つのパラグラフができるように、適切な番号を下の欄に書いてみましょう。書いたら、音声を聞いて確認しましょう。

1. Ichiro said he felt grateful for the opportunity to play in the Major Leagues, and ended his statement by thanking the fans in both the US and Japan for all of their support.

2. He went on to say that he thought it was fitting that his last games as a professional were played in his home country of Japan.

3. In a statement released by the Seattle Mariners, Ichiro said that he felt honored to end his big league career with Seattle, where it started.

4. On March 21, 2019, Ichiro Suzuki announced his retirement from baseball at the Tokyo Dome, where he began his professional baseball career.

B 過去に何かに失敗した時の経験について、それが自分にどのように影響を与え、そこから何を学んだかを書いてみましょう。

Seeking Solutions

　近年、プラスチックごみによる環境破壊が世界的に問題となっており、生態系の破壊や人体への影響が心配されています。このような現状に対して、我々消費者はどのような行動をとるべきなのでしょうか。この Unit では、プラスチックごみ問題の解決に向けた対応についての文章を読み、問題解決に関連する英語表現を身につけましょう。

Warm-Up Questions

次の質問に対して、**1.** では英語で答え、**2.** では適当な答えを選び、☑をつけましょう。

1. What kind of disposable plastic items do you use? (for example, plastic bags)

_____ / _____ / _____ / _____ / _____

2. What's your image of disposable plastic?

☐ Convenient　　☐ Wasteful　　☐ Garbage

☐ Cheap　　☐ Harmful　　☐ Other: _____

Think Twice Before Choosing Plastic

1　Today the world is generating more plastic trash than ever before. Unfortunately, very little of it gets recycled. Plastics are littering our towns and cities, as well as our rivers, lakes and oceans, causing health problems in humans and threatening animal and marine life.　In order
5▶ to solve this problem, we as consumers need to change our mindset and to adopt environmentally sound habits, starting with our plastic consumption.

2　To efficiently reduce plastic waste, there is a need to reduce our usage of plastic. In other words, we need to change our everyday behaviors and not use plastic when there is a better alternative.　Saying no to plastic straws in cafés and restaurants is one
10▶ example.　Another example is to refuse plastic bags at supermarkets and other shops. Currently, some 500 billion plastic bags are produced annually, so bringing cloth shopping bags will greatly reduce this number.　Yet another effective solution is to purchase refills for such products as liquid soap, pens and printer ink.

3　Another way to reduce our usage of plastic is to choose other materials over
15▶ plastic whenever possible.　Steel, bamboo, wood and glass straws are great alternatives to plastic straws and can be reused.　Purchasing products that are packed in cardboard containers such as laundry detergent, beverages and eggs will reduce the amount of plastic that needs to be produced.　Cardboard is easily recycled and, unlike plastic, it's biodegradable.　Choosing products that are made of wood or metal such
20▶ as clothes hangers, storage containers and trash cans will also reduce the demand for plastic.

4　Plastic has made our life convenient in many ways, and it would be hard to imagine a world without it.　However, plastic has also become a global problem, so we need to think twice before choosing it.

Notes　litter ～を散らかす　mindset 考え方　environmentally sound 環境に優しい　alternative 代替手段
refill 詰め替え品　cardboard ダンボール、厚紙　biodegradable 生分解性の

Comprehension Questions

本文の内容に関して、次の質問の答えとして適当なものを選びましょう。

1. What does the passage mainly discuss?

   a. recycling plastic   **b.** reducing plastic   **c.** reusing plastic

2. What is NOT suggested as a material for making straws?

   a. glass   **b.** metal   **c.** paper

3. What advantage does cardboard have over plastic?

   a. It's cheaper.   **b.** It's more easily recycled.   **c.** It's not as heavy.

Guided Summary

39
Audio

本文の語句を使って、次の要約文を完成させましょう。完成したら、音声を聞いて確認しましょう。

Plastic waste is a big problem in the world today. Plastic is ___[1]___ our land and water, causing ___[2]___ problems in people and threatening animal and ___[3]___ life. To help solve this problem, we need to ___[4]___ plastic waste. Saying no to plastic products such as ___[5]___ in restaurants is one way. Buying ___[6]___ for liquid soap, etc. will also help. Another way to reduce plastic usage is to purchase products made from non-plastic ___[7]___, such as metal clothes ___[8]___ and trash cans. Buying things that use ___[9]___ packaging including laundry ___[10]___ and drinks will also reduce the demand for plastic.

目的を表す

(1) 前置詞句で表す

< 前置詞 for ＋名詞 >で「〜のために」「〜のための」という目的の意味を表せます。

- We work **for** the common good.

前置詞 for の直後に動名詞が来る場合は、主に物事の用途や目的を表します。

- This is a useful tool **for** detecting defects.

(2) 不定詞で表す

to 不定詞の副詞的用法で「〜するために」という意味を表せます。

- I'm going to law school **(in order) to** become a corporate lawyer.

(3) so that で表す

so that が導く節で「…が〜するために」という意味を表せます。that は省略されることもあります。

- Please speak up **so that** everyone can hear you.

Check Your Understanding

(　) の中から適切な語句を選び、○で囲みましょう。

1. Sleeping too much is not good (as / for) your health.

2. Security cameras were installed in those areas (to / for) maintain public security.

3. We closed the door (in order to / so that) nobody could hear our conversation.

Sentence Writing

A (　　) 内の指示に従って、次の英文を書き換えてみましょう。

1. This technology was developed in order to prevent illegal copying.

(**for the purpose of** を用いて)

_____

_____

2. We are working hard so that we can win the competition. (**in order to** を用いて)

_____

3. He sat at the back of the classroom in order to watch everyone. (**so that** を用いて)

_____

_____

4. She stepped aside so that they could pass. (**to** 不定詞を用いて)

_____

_____

B 自分で自由に考えて次の英文を完成させましょう。

1. I'm studying at this college in order to _____

_____.

2. I'd like to save money so that _____

_____.

3. I think smartphones are useful for _____

and _____.

4. In order to be successful in life, you need to _____

and _____.

Paragraph Writing

A 次の英文を並べ替えて、１つのパラグラフができるように、適切な番号を下の欄に書いてみましょう。書いたら、音声を聞いて確認しましょう。

1. Paul Fisher, head of Fisher Pen Company, solved this problem by inventing a pen that uses compressed nitrogen to force ink out of the nozzle, instead of using gravity to make it flow.

2. This made it the ideal device for writing in space, as it could write crisp, clean lines while upside down, without the fire and other safety concerns of a pencil.

3. In the early 1960s, the US space program needed a pen that worked in the weightless environment of space.

4. In 1967, after months of testing, NASA bought 400 Space Pens for future missions.

B アメリカ国内の銃による暴力を減らすための対策方法を３つ考え、以下のパラグラフを完成させましょう。

Every year, gun violence results in tens of thousands of deaths and injuries in the United States. How can this number be reduced? _____

_____

_____

_____

_____

_____

_____

_____

Let Me Entertain You

　地名や場所の名前の由来はさまざまです。耳慣れた名前でも、その背後には隠された歴史や逸話が潜んでいることがあります。旅行に出かける際には、訪れる場所の名前の由来も調べてみましょう。ひょっとすると面白いエピソードが隠されているかもしれません。この Unit では、読み手を楽しませる文章に使われている表現を学びましょう。

Warm-Up Questions

次の左側にある有名な場所と最も関連が深いものを右側から選び、線で結びましょう。

Broadway ・ ・ *The American financial markets*

Buckingham Palace ・ ・ *The American film industry*

Hollywood ・ ・ *London or British police*

Scotland Yard ・ ・ *The American high technology sector*

Silicon Valley ・ ・ *American plays and musicals*

Wall Street ・ ・ *The British royal family*

A Well-Kept Secret

1 During the Cold War, spy satellites belonging to the former Soviet Union were aimed at the Washington, D.C. area of the United States. Soviet military experts worked
5▶ around the clock analyzing photographs taken from the satellites, particularly the photos of the Pentagon. Located across the Potomac River from Washington, D.C., the Pentagon is the headquarters of the U.S. Department of Defense. It is the world's largest office building, with more than 25,000 employees. The building is shaped like a five-sided donut, with a large courtyard in the middle.

10▶ **2** One day, some Soviet analysts noticed a curious trend while looking at satellite images of the Pentagon. All day long, from early morning until late in the evening, American military officers of all ranks and areas of expertise would exit the Pentagon and head straight to a building at the center of the courtyard. The officers would enter the building, speak with someone inside, receive something, and then hurry
15▶ away, all in the space of a few minutes.

3 The Soviet analysts examined the photos closely. What kind of highly valuable, top secret information was being exchanged from the "nerve center" of the Pentagon? They made it their top priority to find out what the Americans were up to. Despite their best efforts, however, they were never able to discover the secret.

20▶ **4** As it turns out, the actual purpose of the facility was very important, indeed, one which many of the Pentagon employees depended on each and every day. It was, in a way, a matter of life and death for them. Today, tour guides tell visitors to the Pentagon that it was rumored that Soviet missiles were aimed at that building. And that is why the building earned the nickname Café Ground Zero, the deadliest hot
25▶ dog stand in the world.

Notes   spy satellite 偵察衛星   work around the clock 休みなく働く   headquarters 本部   courtyard 中庭
area of expertise 専門分野   nerve center 中枢   rumor 噂をする

Comprehension Questions

本文の内容に関して、次の質問の答えとして適当なものを選びましょう。

1. What is the Pentagon?

    a. a spy satellite   **b.** a U.S. Department of Defense building   **c.** a courtyard

2. What were the Soviet analysts hoping to find in the photographs?

    a. government information   **b.** a secret passage
    c. the Pentagon "nerve center"

3. What did the "nerve center" of the Pentagon turn out to be?

    a. a post office   **b.** a visitor information center   **c.** a hot dog stand

Guided Summary

42 Audio

本文の語句を使って、次の要約文を完成させましょう。完成したら、音声を聞いて確認しましょう。

During the Cold War, Soviet spy ___(1)___ took photographs of the Washington, D.C. area, particularly the Pentagon, the ___(2)___ of the U.S. Department of Defense. Analysts came to notice that throughout each day, American ___(3)___ officers would leave the Pentagon, enter a building in the ___(4)___, briefly talk to someone, and then ___(5)___ a small package. Thinking that the packages contained highly valuable, ___(6)___ information, the analysts tried unsuccessfully to ___(7)___ the secret. Today, tour guides tell ___(8)___ to the Pentagon that Soviet ___(9)___ may have been aimed at that small building, which turned out to be no more than a ___(10)___ stand.

Writing Strategy

(1) 分詞構文で表す

分詞が副詞句として用いられる構文を分詞構文といい、付帯状況（「〜しながら」「〜で」「〜して、そして」）や時（「〜するとき」）を表すことができます。

- Sean slammed the door, **making a loud noise**.
- **Founded in 1955**, the museum began to collect artwork by local artists.

(2) 接続詞で表す（while, when など）

副詞節の主語と主節の主語が同一の場合、副詞節内の主語と be 動詞はしばしば省略されます。

- You should not use a smartphone **while (you are) walking**.
- The accident happened **when I was watching TV**.

(3) ＜ with ＋ O ＋ C ＞で表す

＜ with ＋ O ＋ C ＞で「…が〜（の状態）で」という意味の付帯状況を表すことができます。O は名詞、C は（現在／過去）分詞、形容詞、副詞、前置詞句のいずれかです。

- Ken was singing **with his eyes closed**.
- Josh rushed into the meeting room **with his hat on**.
- Sue spoke to me **with tears in her eyes**.

Check Your Understanding

（　）の中から適切な語句を選び、○で囲みましょう。

1. (Holding / Held) a mirror in her left hand, Melanie cut her own hair.

2. Edith looked at me (with / while) a smile on her face.

3. Dustin was standing still with his arms (folding / folded).

Sentence Writing

A　(　　　) 内の指示に従って、次の英文を書き換えてみましょう。

1.　I was almost hit by a car while I was walking to school.（省略できる語句を省略して）

_____

_____

2.　You cannot drink alcohol during pregnancy.（**while** を用いて）

_____

3.　They kept staring at me, which made me uncomfortable.（**making** を用いて）

_____

_____

4.　You shouldn't speak when your mouth is full of food.（**with** を用いて）

_____

B　次の語句を並び換えて、次の英文を完成させましょう。

1.　roads / snowed / all / heavily / impassable / night / making

It _____, _____

_____.

2.　friends / big / face / with / greeted / on / a / her / her / smile

Susan _____

_____.

3.　foreign / popular / by / travel / millions / is / destination / of / a / tourists

Visited _____ annually, Japan _____

_____.

Paragraph Writing

A 次の英文を並べ替えて、1つのパラグラフができるように、適切な番号を下の欄に書いてみましょう。書いたら、音声を聞いて確認しましょう。

1. "Every time you misbehave, one of my hairs turns gray," she went on to explain.

2. The mother, trying to use the occasion to teach her son the importance of good behavior, answered, "It's because of you, Billy."

3. One day, a curious child named Billy asked his mother why some of her hairs were gray.

4. Upon hearing this, Billy replied innocently, "Oh, so that's why grandma has only gray hairs on her head."

B 自分自身の経験をもとに、人を楽しませるような話（恐怖体験、面白いエピソード、恥ずかしかった話など）を書いてみましょう。

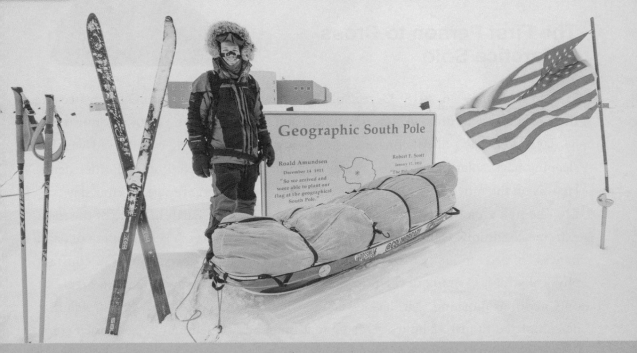

　歴史に刻まれるような偉業は、人に夢と感動、そして希望や勇気を与えてくれるものです。たいていの場合、そのような偉業が成し遂げられるまでの道のりは平坦ではありません。この Unit では、アメリカの冒険家コリン・オブレイディが世界で初めて達成した偉業についてのエッセイを読み、人を奮い立たせるような文章に使われている表現を学びましょう。

Warm-Up Questions

次の左側にある人物が持つ世界初の記録を右側から選び、線で結びましょう。

Chiaki Mukai　　　　　　·

Christopher Columbus　·

Edmund Hillary　　　　·

Ferdinand Magellan　　·

Wright brothers　　　　·

· *First pilots*

· *First Japanese woman in space*

· *First to reach the top of Mount Everest*

· *First to repeatedly explore the New World*

· *First to sail around the world*

The First Person to Cross Antarctica Solo

1   On December 26, 2018, 33-year-old American adventurer Colin O'Brady became the first person to cross Antarctica unassisted. He made the 1,500-km journey in 54 days. O'Brady pulled along a sled of heavy gear containing a tent, cold-weather sleeping bags, solar panels, skis, a satellite phone, freeze-dried food and other items.
5▸ He was on the move for 12 hours on most days, covering on average 30 km a day.

2   The trek took O'Brady across the coldest continent on Earth in some of the most extreme conditions. He lost so much weight that his wristwatch kept slipping off, and he was "scared" to look at his unclothed body. After nearly two months of constant physical strain, O'Brady decided to make the final push as he was making breakfast
10▸ on Christmas morning. The last leg was particularly difficult—a 120-km stretch that he completed in just 32 hours. During that time, he stopped only once to melt some ice, eat a big dinner and call his wife.

3   In finishing, O'Brady defeated another adventurer, 49-year-old Louis Rudd, who was attempting the same crossing at the same time. Before starting out, the two close
15▸ friends met at a hotel bar in Chile and agreed to turn their separate attempts to cross Antarctica solo and unaided by wind into a formal competition. The two men came from very different backgrounds. O'Brady had raced in triathlons before climbing each of the Seven Summits—the highest peaks on every continent. Rudd, on the other hand, was a British Army Captain who was given leave from the military in
20▸ order to train and attempt the crossing. O'Brady ended up finishing the race several days ahead of his friend, his accomplishment nothing short of amazing. It was a lonely effort marked by long days, short nights and remarkable endurance—a truly inspiring journey.

Notes Antarctica 南極大陸   sled そり   last leg 最後の行程   accomplishment 偉業
nothing short of まさに〜に他ならない   endurance 忍耐力

Comprehension Questions

本文の内容に関して、次の質問の答えとして適当なものを選びましょう。

1. What is one of the difficulties O'Brady faced during his journey?

    a. weight loss   **b.** a broken leg   **c.** shortage of food

2. Which of the following things did O'Brady NOT do during the final stretch?

    a. eat   **b.** sleep   **c.** make a phone call

3. Who was Louis Rudd?

    a. an American adventurer   **b.** a British military man   **c.** a Chilean bar owner

Guided Summary

 45 Audio

本文の語句を使って、次の要約文を完成させましょう。完成したら、音声を聞いて確認しましょう。

A 33-year-old __¹_____ named Colin O'Brady became the first

person to cross the Antarctic __²_____ in 2018. The 1,500-km

journey took __³_____ days. O'Brady pulled a sled of heavy __⁴_____ for

about 12 hours each day. He completed the last __⁵_____ of his trip, a 120-

km stretch, in only 32 hours, stopping only __⁶_____ to melt some ice,

eat dinner and call his __⁷_____. O'Brady defeated his friend and fellow

adventurer Louis Rudd, a 49-year-old British Army __⁸_____, who

was __⁹_____ the same crossing at the same time. O'Brady's

inspiring journey was one marked by loneliness, long days, short nights and

remarkable __¹⁰_____.

Writing Strategy

感情を表現する

(1) 形容詞で表す

afraid（恐れて）、glad（喜んで）、proud（誇りに思って）、sorry（気の毒に思って）などの感情を表す形容詞は人を主語にとり、物事を主語とすることができません。

- Everyone is **proud** of his achievements.

(2) 過去分詞で表す

心理的に影響を与える意味の他動詞の過去分詞形は、人の感情を表す形容詞としてよく用いられます。bored（退屈した）、disappointed（がっかりした）、interested（興味を持った）、scared（怖がって）、surprised（驚いて）などがあります。

- I'm very **disappointed** in you.

心理的に影響を与える意味の他動詞の現在分詞形は、感情をもたらす原因となるものの性質を表すことに注意しましょう。

- I'm **surprised** at the news.

- The news is **surprising**.

Check Your Understanding

(　) の中から適切な語句を選び、○で囲みましょう。

1. Susan looked (shocking / shocked) at the news.

2. I am really (pleasant / pleased) to hear that.

3. His explanation was (confusing / confused).

Sentence Writing

A (   ) 内の指示に従って、次の英文を書き換えてみましょう。

1. I'm very interested in the book. (**interesting** を用いて)

_____

2. His success amazed everyone. (**everyone** を主語にして)

_____

3. I'm surprised that Judy quit the company. (**It is surprising** で始めて)

_____

_____

4. I'm afraid that I will fail again. (**afraid of** を用いて)

_____

B 自分で自由に考えて次の英文を完成させましょう。

1. I'm very interested in _____,

but I'm not interested in _____ at all.

2. I'll be surprised if _____

_____.

3. I'm afraid of _____ and

_____.

4. I feel excited when _____

_____.

Paragraph Writing

A 次の英文を並べ替えて、1つのパラグラフができるように、適切な番号を下の欄に書いてみましょう。書いたら、音声を聞いて確認しましょう。

46
Audio

1. J.K. Rowling got the idea for Harry Potter during a train ride in 1990.

2. What makes Rowling's story so inspiring is that, despite all of the problems she faced, she never gave up her dream of telling the world a story about the magical life of Harry Potter.

3. During the seven years that it took her to finish the book, her mother died, she got divorced, and she lived in near poverty.

4. And if that wasn't enough, her book was rejected by no fewer than 12 publishers.

B あなたに刺激を与えてくれる人(家族、歴史上の人物、有名人、アスリートなど)について、その人がどういう人で、なぜ刺激を受けているかについて書いてみましょう。

The person who inspires me most is _____

_____

_____

_____

_____

_____

_____

_____

_____

クラス用音声CD有り（別売）

Jigsaw—Insightful Reading to Successful Writing

パラグラフのパターン別に学んで磨く英語力

2020年1月20日　初版発行
2024年1月20日　第 4 刷

著　者　Robert Hickling / 八島 純

発行者　松村達生

発行所　センゲージ ラーニング株式会社

　　　　〒102-0073　東京都千代田区九段北1-11-11　第2フナトビル5階
　　　　電話 03-3511-4392
　　　　FAX 03-3511-4391
　　　　e-mail: eltjapan@cengage.com
　　　　copyright © 2020 センゲージ ラーニング株式会社

装丁・組版　　藤原志麻（クリエイド・ラーニング株式会社）

編集協力　　　クリエイド・ラーニング株式会社

本文イラスト　大塚砂織

印刷・製本　　株式会社エデュプレス

ISBN 978-4-86312-369-4